CURRE]
LANGUAGE AND
CULTURE STUDIES

CURRENT TRENDS IN LANGUAGE AND CULTURE STUDIES

Selected Proceedings of the 20th Southeast Conference on
Foreign Languages, Literatures, and Film

DeLand, Florida. March 2-3, 2012

Edited by

**Yves-Antoine Clemmen, Margit Grieb,
and Will Lehman**

Brown Walker Press
Boca Raton

Current Trends in Language and Culture Studies: Selected Proceedings of the 20th Southeast Conference on Foreign Languages, Literatures, and Film

BrownWalker Press
Boca Raton, Florida • USA
2013

ISBN-10: 1-61233-672-8
ISBN-13: 978-1-61233-672-5

www.brownwalker.com

Cover image © Can Stock Photo Inc. / 4ustudio

Library of Congress Cataloging-in-Publication Data

Southeast Conference on Foreign Languages, Literatures, and Film
(20th : 2012 : DeLand, Fla.)
  Current trends in language and culture studies : selected
proceedings of the 20th Southeast Conference on Foreign Languages,
Literatures, and Film / edited by Yves-Antoine Clemmen, Margit
Grieb, and Will Lehman.
     pages cm
  Includes bibliographical references.
  ISBN-13: 978-1-61233-672-5 (pbk. : alk. paper)
  ISBN-10: 1-61233-672-8 (pbk. : alk. paper)
   1. Literature--History and criticism--Congresses. 2. Foreign films--
History and criticism--Congresses. 3. Culture in literature--
Congresses. 4. Culture in motion pictures--Congresses. I. Clemmen,
Yves-Antoine, 1961- editor of comilation. II. Grieb, Margit, editor of
compilation. III. Lehman, Will, editor of compilation. IV. Title.
  PN33.S67 2013
  809--dc23   2013003485

TABLE OF CONTENTS

INTRODUCTION

Since 1983 the Southeast Conference on Foreign Languages, Literatures, and Film (SCFLLF) has been a showcase for scholarship in the Humanities with a special emphasis on non-English language area studies. Various universities located in central Florida, i.e. the University of Central Florida, Rollins College, and Stetson University, have hosted the conference over the past couple of decades, but since 2010 Stetson University and the University of South Florida in Tampa are exclusive hosts to the bi-annual SCFLLF meetings.[1]

In 2012 the 20th Southeast Conference on Foreign Languages, Literatures, and Film attracted again close to seventy national and international scholars presenting their research on language, literature, film, culture, and pedagogy. The conference featured 21 sessions and convened on the Stetson University campus in DeLand, Florida on March 2-3, 2012, and it was generously supported by the Stetson University Department of Modern Languages and the Stetson University Department of Continuing Education. We were especially fortunate to have had William O'Connor provide administrative assistance as well as the support of our colleagues who, in addition to attending conference sessions, also organized and moderated various sessions. We would also like to thank the Department of World Languages at USF for financial support for this publication.

The keynote address of the 2012 SCFLLF "Grand Guignol: French Theater of Horror from the Belle Epoque" was delivered by author Agnès Pierron on a uniquely French brand of theater: the Grand Guignol. The Grand Guignol's existence spans six decades, from 1897 till it closed its doors permanently in 1962. It is also a very geographically restricted genre of theater since it rarely ventured outside of one small venue at the bottom of impasse Chaptal in the both famous and infamous neighborhood of Pigalle, Paris. It had its heyday in the 20s and 30s but never entirely recovered from the effects of the Second World War, as if the horrors presented on stage could not compete any longer with what had happened in

---

[1] The 2010 post-conference publication including selected proceedings is entitled *Cultural Perspectives on Film, Literature, and Language* (Brown-Walker Press, 2010) and co-edited by Will Lehman and Margit Grieb.

reality. Nearly vanished into artistic oblivion, the Grand Guignol theatre has recently found new interest with theater companies based in the United States, and Agnès Pierron's work is the main source of information and the most complete available repertoire of that theater in print.

Agnés Pierron was originally trained in acting at the Conservatory of Nancy where she received a *premier prix de comédie*. As a researcher she contributed to several encyclopedias, such as Larousse and Bordas, and to specialized journals, such as *L'avant-scène* or *Le journal de la Comédie Française*. From 1981 till 1985 Dr. Pierron was engaged in acting as well as part of the artistic board of directors of La Criée, the National Theatre of Marseille. She later returned to research working on different collections of the great French lexicographic endeavors of Le Robert, one of the best known French dictionaries. She compiled the *Dictionnaire de citations sur les personnages célèbres* (Dictionary of Quotations on Famous Characters), as well as the *Dictionnaire de la langue du théâtre* (Dictionary of Theatre Terms) which received the *Prix de la critique* (from the Syndicate of Theatre, Dance and Music Criticism) in 2003. She published two other specialty dictionaries, the *Dictionnaire de la langue du cirque* (Dictionary of Circus Terms) (2003) and the *Dictionnaire des mots du sexe* (Dictionary of Sex Vocabulary) (2010) with the *Éditions Balland* where she also directs the collections "Les Dicos d'Agnès."

She is, however, especially well known as the world specialist of the French horror theater Grand Guignol with three seminal works of reference on the subject: *Le Grand Guignol, le théâtre des peurs de la Belle Epoque* (collection "Bouquins" chez Robert Laffont, 1995), *Les Nuits Blanches du Grand-Guignol* (Seuil, 2002), and *Maxa, la femme la plus assassinée du monde* (L'entretemps, 2011). Agnès Pierron was the first to rediscover and investigate this theater that had fallen into oblivion, and she has been lecturing on this topic since the late 1990's, thereby contributing to the rediscovery of this uniquely French theatre. We thank Dr. Pierron for her captivating keynote address, as well as the panelists for their thought-provoking contributions, all of which made the 2012 SCFLLF conference a memorable and stimulating event, and a bellwether for future conferences.

In previous editions of selected SCFLLF conference proceedings the editors opted for a language-oriented organization of the publication. This year, a theme-oriented arrangement is better suited to accommodate the selection of contributions. Hence, we have elected to divide *Current Trends in Language and Culture Studies* into four clusters containing similarly themed essays.

The first and largest section of our collection contains contributions by Stephan K. Schindler, Carine Mardorossian, Christine McCall Probes and Martine Le Glaunec Landis, Silvia Baage, and Sophie Boyer and discusses the various approaches to and challenges involved in representing violence and trauma in literature and film. In his essay "Limits of Representation: Documenting the Holocaust," Stephan K. Schindler argues that documentary films about the Holocaust, despite the genre's claim to historical authenticity and objectivity, become entangled in established audio-visual and narrative conventions of the medium film and the institution of the cinema. Citing early and recent documentaries, Schindler demonstrates how filmmakers cannot escape their own ideological context, the medium's preoccupation with narratives about the individual, as well as the Nazi's propagandistic shaping of the iconography of the Holocaust.

Schindler's essay is followed by Carine Mardorossian's "Violence, contingence, et inégalité sexuelle chez Maryse Condé." In her essay, Mardorossian focuses on the contingent dimensions of power relations in Guadeloupean writer Maryse Condé's fiction, which, she argues, are emphasized without obscuring their violating and traumatizing effects. In *Who Slashed Célanire's Throat?* in particular, Condé's representation reveals that the supposedly discrete identities in the name of which violence is often perpetuated are no less oppressive when they are imbricated in a hybridizing dynamic. In so doing, her fiction challenges postcolonial studies' overly celebratory endorsement of hybridizing ethics. Likewise, Silvia Baage also considers postcolonial discourse and the issue of violence in her "Mediterranean and French Caribbean Paroxysms: Marie Ferranti's Violent Discourse about Corsica." The author compares and contrasts the function of violence in contemporary postcolonial island discourses of Corsica and the French Caribbean archipelago to situate her analysis of Marie Ferranti's *La Fuite aux Agriates* (2000). Although this novel can be read as a rewriting of Prosper Mérimée's *Carmen* from a Corsican perspective, depicting gendered violence and terror from a female viewpoint, Baage's analysis contextualizes Ferranti's violent discourse by illustrating that the representation of Corsican island space with its culture, history, and society, is a salient contribution to the body of French-speaking literature in French and Francophone studies.

Christine McCall Probes and Martine Le Glaunec Landis discuss in their joint contribution the representation of violence in literature of 16th-century France. They examine the remembrance of the violence of the French Renaissance, specifically around the Saint Bartholomew's Day Massacre in 1572, in Pierre Matthieu's *La Guisiade* (1589), an important dramatization of the time. In their essay entitled "The Taste of Violence: Senses, Signs, Biblical and Theological Allusion in the Service of the Dramatization of History: Pierre Matthieu's *Guisiade*," the authors discover and analyze rhetorical strategies which heighten and memorialize for the stage the taste of violence manifest in the historical acts and records. Finally, Sophie Boyer's "Le roman familial des Jardin: pour une psychanalyse de l'écriture-miroir d'Alexandre Jardin" returns the discussion to contemporary literary confrontations with acts of violence. Boyer's essay demonstrates how Alexandre Jardin's latest work, *Des gens très bien* (2011), can be interpreted as a twofold project. It consists, firstly, of the rewriting of his previous novel, *Le roman des Jardin* (2005), and, as such, offers an inverted echo of both the novel's thematic and narrative structure. It serves, secondly, as a confession of his family's dark secret, namely the direct responsibility of his grand-father, Jean Jardin, for the Vel' d'Hiv' Roundup that led to the deportation of thousands of French Jews in 1942.

In Section II we present four essays that deal with topics addressing identity, subjectivity, and the national in a variety of literary and dramatic works. In the first contribution, entitled "El teatro vanguardista centroamericano inaugural: performatividad e identidad en *Cuculcán y Chinfonía burguesa*," Alessandra Chiriboga Holzheu introduces and contextualizes two avant-garde plays that construct and perform divergent types of national imagined communities. While both adhere to cultural *mestizaje,* one play models a catholic-based identity while the other portrays Mayan-based cultural distinctiveness. In a similar fashion as the manifesto, these two plays perform divergent and unique models of the avant-garde aesthetic used as a means to publicly address, provoke, and shape modernized national subjectivities and legitimize the writer's social role within these imagined communities. Jessica Burke, in the subsequent essay "Body, Identity, and the Writing Process in the Narrative of Carmen Boullosa," also discusses issues of identity in the Central-American context. She examines the narrative prose of contemporary Mexican author Carmen Boullosa, focusing on the relationship between body, identity, and writing in Boullosa's novels. By exploring the relationship between characters' bodies, their sense of self, and the text that contains them, Burke argues that Boullosa's fragmented narrative allows for reconfiguration of physical and textual bodies, and of identity. It is through dismantling instituted notions of gender, identity, body, and narrative that Boullosa creates a space for reinvention of the self, and of novelistic form.

In "The Literature of Terror: Sadur's Gothic-Fantastic Fictions" Tatyana Novikov offers a contribution concerned with the interconnectedness of identity and the nation in the context of contemporary Russia. She examines Gothic elements in the writings of Nina Sadur, a major figure in Russian prose. Reading her fiction as part of the Gothic tradition allows a vision of a dark universe, where evil is unpredictable and pandemonium underlies the surface of everyday life. Novikov argues that Sadur's Gothic fiction articulates collective anxieties about the integrity of the nation and the dissolution of order, meaning, and identity in the post-Soviet era. Terry Cochran's "The Materiality of Mind in Stefan Zweig's *Chess Story*," by contrast, highlights the relationship between the mind and historical continuity rather than emphasizing the connectedness of subjectivity to the national. In reflecting on Stephan Zweig's *Chess Story*, Terry Cochran examines the underlying thoughts about the intimate link between mind and matter in Zweig's novella as the vehicle for human consciousness.

Section III considers representations of race and gender in literature and film and includes contributions on works by Italian, German, and French authors and directors in the first half of the 20th century. This section begins with Joanne Frallicciardi Lyon's essay entitled "The Trials of Motherhood in Laudomia Bonanni's 'Il fosso'," in which the author investigates conceptions of motherhood in Fascist and wartime Italy. Lyon's analysis brings to light the influence of patriarchal institutions in shaping motherhood and argues that the seeds of many important Bonannian themes such as gender restrictions, the mother-son bond, and the weak head of household find their origin in this short story. Whereas Lyon focuses on representations involving motherhood, Aneka Meier explores the depiction of young single 'working girls' during the interwar years in Germany reflecting the tensions and ambiguity, as well as the transitional character of the Weimar Republic. Her "All the Single Ladies: 'Working Girls' in Weimar Germany" draws from literature, film, and images in popular 1920s magazines. Meier discusses how traditional gender roles and expectations collided with the propagation of female independence and the pursuit of women's sexual fulfillment.

Mary Sanders Pollock's "An Unnatural History of Species in the fiction of Vercors and Laurence Gonzales" concludes the third section of this collection with a contribution addressing discourses of race and ethnicity. She argues that Vercors' *Les animaux dénaturés* (1953), a fable in which species serves as a metaphor for race and ethnicity, is newly relevant as a literal examination of species as an issue in itself. According to Pollock, like many more recent works, including *Lucy* (2010) by Laurence Gonzales, Vercors' novel calls into question the validity of rigid boundaries (race, species, gender) set into place for the purpose of social and political domination.

Whereas the first three sections of *Current Trends in Language and Culture Studies* focus on various themes manifest in literature, film, and culture, the contributions in the collection's final section seek to illuminate important and effective strategies for language learning and teaching as well as approaches for including culture into the humanities curriculum in higher education. In "Instructional Units Informed by Backward Design," Eva Maria Russo acknowledges the durable individuality of teachers' classroom practices and the importance of an un-teachable enthusiastic personality but argues that clear guidelines are nonetheless available for those training graduate student instructors in a "post-method" age. Russo points to sources, such as the proficiency goals provided by ACTFL and the CEFR to the curriculum development template provided by Wiggins and McTighe's *Understanding by Design*, in which instructors find a clear framework to guide their teaching. These sources help focus teachers' selection of highly contextualized materials and guide the creation of plans that facilitate both students' accurate comprehension of subject matter and successfully scaffolded production of the target language. Gabriel Ignacio Barreneche expands the discussion of language pedagogy to include the classroom beyond the traditional campus space in his contribution "Achieving the LEAP Report's Essential Learning Outcomes through Service-learning in Foreign Language Pedagogy." He examines how foreign language programs can use service-learning and effective partnerships with local community agencies not only to increase students' linguistic skills, but also to prepare them for the challenges of a global society and enhance their intercultural and ethical competencies.

We conclude section IV and the volume with a contribution by Heike Scharm entitled "From Analytical to Analogous Thinking: The

Relevance of Transnational Approaches." She expands the discussions of language pedagogy to the broader field of teaching in the humanities by making an appeal for devising interdisciplinary and multicultural curricula in the humanities. Referring to examples in philosophy, sociology, and literature, she highlights the discrepancy between our changing global reality on one hand, and our traditionally "inward" Western education and thought on the other. Scharm proposes that analogous models of thought shift the focus from interiority and uniqueness to exteriority and correspondence, thus promoting a better understanding of the self and the other, while fostering a mentality of global community builders.

Unfortunately the editors were not able to accommodate all of the conference presentations at the 20th Southeast Conference on Foreign Languages, Literatures, and Film nor the entirety of papers submitted for inclusion in this collection. The editors hope that their selection of papers will invite productive debates among scholars within the various fields showcased and stimulate further interest in the myriad of topics discussed herein. We look forward to another successful SCFFLF in 2014 which will be hosted by the University of South Florida in Tampa.

Yves Clemmen, Stetson University

Margit Grieb, University of South Florida

Will Lehman, Western Carolina University

I: VIOLENCE AND TRAUMA IN LITERATURE AND FILM

Limits of Representation: Documenting the Holocaust

Stephan K. Schindler

Since the surprising success of the fictional NBC mini-series *Holocaust* (1978) and subsequently Steven Spielberg's feature film *Schindler's List* (1993) in educating the post-memory public about the traumas of an unprecedented genocide, visual representations of the Holocaust have been scrutinized with regard to their ethical and aesthetical appropriateness.[1] Many critics and historians have voiced their reservations whether popular media and classical Hollywood genres are capable of depicting historical events authentically without evoking melodramatic sentimentality or scopophilic desire usually associated with narrative film. Traditional narrative film, with its powerful construction of fictional worlds, its distraction from the "real world" via fantasy, and its alluring images, seems rather unsuitable to tell the story of genocide. Narrative films' inability to free itself from conventions and form might provoke Theodor W. Adorno's famous dictum "to write poetry after Auschwitz is barbaric," (Adorno 30),[2] because an "aesthetic" response to Auschwitz seems to transfigure the real suffering of its victims into an object of aesthetic (dis-)pleasure. The incomprehensible enormity of the Shoah appears incompatible with the Western artistic tradition; it evokes the limits of aesthetic concepts and renders art trivial. Nazi concentration camps constitute such a terrific assault on religious, humanistic, moral, and philosophical values that narratives emerging from or propagating ethical standards become speechless vis-à-vis the factual horror of extreme genocide. The entire aura of negativity that surrounds the historic event—a story that cannot be told because it contains unimaginable horrors—has even culminated in the calling

---

[1] A comprehensive summary of this discussion can be found in Ginsberg, pp. 1-59.
[2] German original: „[...] nach Auschwitz ein Gedicht zu schreiben, ist barbarisch [...]."

for an altogether prohibition of images (*Bilderverbot*).[3] That is why some critics have argued that only documentary films should be permitted to depict the Holocaust, because —so goes the argument—only a genre that seemingly adheres to the discourse of sobriety would be able to guarantee some level of authenticity and would allow the viewer to remain in critical and reflective distance.

In times of historical amnesia and the postmodern collapse of historical consciousness there seems to be a greater demand for Holocaust representations which are disseminated in media that might challenge the authority of traditional historiography. Michael Rothberg argues that there is "a demand for documentation, a demand for reflection on the formal limits of representation, and a demand for the risky public circulation of discourses on the event" (Rothberg 7). However, one of the representational problems of narrating the story of the genocide derives from the fact that, unlike other historic genocides, the Holocaust has been painstakingly documented by the perpetrators themselves. Relying on these visual documentations, as does Alain Resnais's film essay *Nuit et Brouillard* (*Night and Fog*, 1955) or more recently Yael Hersonski's *A Film Unfinished* (2010), poses the question whether the "typical" images of the Holocaust, what Inga Clendinnen has termed the "identikit image of 'the Holocaust' we carry in our heads" (Clendinnen 165)— depictions of roundups, deportation, concentration camps, slave labor behind barbed wires, killings, burying the dead in mass graves— continue to carry their racist connotations. After all, the visual framing of these processes, aspects, and symbols of the Holocaust has its ideological frame embedded: the narrative anonymity of the victims, degrading camera angles, close-ups of distortion, segregating emphasis on striped uniforms or the Star of David, etc. reveal compositions that utilize cinematographic properties to construct a powerful anti-Semitic or inhuman imagery. [4] Even docu-dramas such as Heinz Schirk's *Die Wannsee Konferenz* (*The Wannsee Conference*, 1984)—the reenactment of the administrative process of the "final solution"— present the victims only within the perpetrators' inhuman discourse where Jews are only mentioned as numbers, in cynical racist anec-

---

[3] For example Claude Lanzmann as discussed by Stuart Liebman in "Introduction" in *Claude Lanzmann's SHOAH*, 5-24. See the critical response to such an absolute position by LaCapra, 95-138.

[4] For the connection between visual framing and ideological frame see Koch, *Die Einstellung ist die Einstellung*.

dotes, or as logistical problems in the process of industrialized killing. Dominick LaCapra has pointed out the hazards of using the perpetrators' views, images, or language which might also reenact the "negative sublime" of their ideology (LaCapra, *History*, 2). Looking at a selected few documentary films of the Holocaust, I would like to address these fundamental questions that arise with Holocaust representations: How does one tell whose story, for what purpose, using what kind of audiovisual composition?

Memory of the Camps, one of the first documentaries on the subject, was produced by the British Ministry of Information in 1945, co-directed by Alfred Hitchcock, and reissued by PBS Frontline in 1985. This film about the liberation of the concentration camps Bergen-Belsen and Buchenwald is considered a masterpiece or even as Annette Insdorf claims "the most authentic and affecting film on the Holocaust" (Insdorf 199-200). It was made to confront the Germans immediately after the war with the atrocities committed by the Nazis and to convince them to accept Allied justice and ideology. However, the film was never finished and fell victim to occupational political strife between the individual Allied factions. It was not shown to the public until its rediscovery in the 1980s.[5] However, the film, had it been shown earlier, might have experienced the same defying reception as other re-education films produced by the Allies such as the American film *Death Mills*: the German public, in comments after viewing *Death Mills*, either distanced themselves from any responsibility for the atrocities or compared the suffering of camp victims with their own in times of Allied bombings. Famous British director Alfred Hitchcock, who is credited with some aspects of the editorial composition of *Memory of the Camps*, was aware of the difficulty of achieving a specific response in viewers. When contemplating the audiovisual composition, to make the documentary more "real" and believable, he suggested "to avoid all tricky editing," to use long shots "which panned [...] from the guards onto the corpses," and to insert a montage of the victims' possessions and body parts such as hair, wedding rings, spectacles, etc. (Gladstone in Haggith 56). Hitchcock, a fiction filmmaker par excellence, was aware of the tools of the trade and how to use editing strategies to allow the recordings to appear more "true" and convincing.

---

[5] Kay Gladstone, "Separate Intentions: The Allied Screening of Concentration Camp Documentaries in Defeated Germany in 1945-46: *Death Mills* and *Memory of the Camps*," in Haggith, 50-64.

Memory of the Camps's opening sequence reveals its careful staging of history and its pedagogical impetus by using Nazi propaganda footage of party meetings and parades and replacing some of the original sound, such as Hitler's voice in speeches, with a voice-over narrating the Nazi rise to power in the fashion of a historical documentary. The film then cuts to a peaceful country still life, replete with trees, farmland, women and children, thus evoking the German notion of "Heimat" (homeland), a concept originating in the 19th century which was re-appropriated as a German value by the Nazis. This pastoral sequence is juxtaposed with images depicting the horrors of the Bergen-Belsen concentration camp. The omnipotent narrator provides a transition for these competing series of images by saying that the intruding non-visible smell of the camp contaminates the beauty of the landscape for the invading Allied troops. What follows is a carefully composed liberation story with images depicting the role benevolent victorious Allied forces played, the dreadful bodies and empty faces of tormented survivors, piles of contorted nude corpses, and the nervously guilty or defiant expressions of perpetrators and bystanders.[6] The film tells a story about the infrastructural challenges of liberating and dismantling a camp, disposing of the dead and caring for the survivors, and it concludes with footage from other camps in order to depict the systematic plan and execution of this unimaginable mass murder. At times the voice-over even remarks on the psychological trauma to which the troops were subjected. Similar images of starved and decaying corpses being buried in mass graves by former German guards are repeated several times. The film seems to linger on the agonizing imagery depicting the liberators having to compound the atrocities by having to dispose of the corpses in a dehumanizing way: they are dragged through sand, hosted onto trucks, and thrown or bulldozed into pits.

With these images the film reveals astounding representational problems. The filmic material is used less for bringing to light the victims' plight and fate than for ideological purposes, namely to provide a screen for identification with the victorious Allied forces, that is to enhance the film's purpose as a re-education tool. The voice-over listing the number of inmates in various camps and a series of shots of mass grave markers generalize individual fates and reduce victims to anonymous statistics. This is highly problematic as this

---

[6] An account for the film's creation can be found in Toby Haggith, "Filming the Liberation of Bergen-Belsen," 33-49.

narrative strategy reproduces an obsession with numbers of Jewish victims akin to the Nazis, most memorable in the administrative detachment of the German officers and politicians discussing the elimination of Europe's Jewish population at the infamous Wannsee Conference. Conversely, the perpetrators are identified as individuals through close-ups showing distinct faces, mentioning of names, and giving interviews while the camera seemingly exploits the nameless victims' nude bodies. In one sequence, *Memory of the Camps* probes the limits of representation, if not to say oversteps them, when complementing the repeated images of female corpses with those of naked bathing women who have survived Bergen-Belsen. The sequence is problematic on several levels. For one, it alludes to a well-known Nazi mass murder deception strategy, when the victims were told they would take showers when in reality they were being gassed to death (Steven Spielberg will later use a similar scene for suspense purposes in *Schindler's List*). While the narrating voice uses this scene as evidence of the falseness of Nazi propaganda disseminating that Jews were dirty, the voyeuristic gaze of the camera lingers and exploits the nakedness of the female body. This sequence raises the question whether these shots are necessary or appropriate in the documentation of the Holocaust, whether they indeed "restore their [the former prisoners'] sense of dignity and humanity" (Haggith, 45), or whether they just reveal the cameraman's desire. The film thus deals with an ethical dilemma of representational crisis: how can the victimized human body continue to be depicted in the aesthetic framework of an established cultural tradition that ends with the Nazi assault on humanity? With the occurrence and depiction of thousands of corpses the famous statue of Laokoon can no longer serve as the classical symbol of human suffering.[7] In other words, the bathing scenes, the display of the individual healthy female body, cannot have a healing or cathartic effect any longer to serve as a remedy for the viewer to overcome the traumatic experience of witnessing the results of mass murder. Such a return to modern aesthetics would deny the fact that the Holocaust has eradicated exactly those philosophical paradigms that could not prevent the genocide in the first place and continues to have epistemological difficulties to explain it.

The image's power of deception is one reason why Claude Lanzmann's monumental 9½ hour masterpiece *Shoah* (1985) avoids

---

[7] See Liliane Weissberg, "In Plain Sight," in: Zelizer, 13-27.

focusing on the perpetrators' perspective or any historical imagery altogether.[8] Instead, his interviews with survivors, former guards, and onlookers reconstruct, in detail, the horrific process of extermination and thus negate the myth of the "unspeakable." Visiting the railway tracks and sites of Auschwitz, Treblinka, and Chelmno in the 1980s, the survivors in Lanzmann's film recall what happened to human beings, whereas the perpetrators and bystanders articulate their terrible detachment using the rhetoric of repression and denial. Lanzmann refuses to let any historical imagery interfere with the voices of the survivors and forces the audience to imagine what these voices describe. Following the classical narrative formula of historical novels, these personal stories make the public history of the Holocaust transparent for an audience which for some time has felt quite comfortable with shelving the memory of the Jewish genocide in abstract histories. Instead of freezing the event in the anonymity of the murder of six million Jews, Lanzmann uses auto-biographical accounts of the Holocaust to re-humanize the vast number of victims by facilitating an understanding of individual physical and psychological suffering. Their testimonies express grief over lost ones and attempt to restore singular identities of victims through giving them names and personal voices. Like Lanzmann, some critics assert that the truth of the Holocaust can only be transmitted through the recordings of survivors' testimony (for example in the ongoing testimonial archive projects at the Universities of Michigan, Southern California or South Florida). Nonetheless, survivor stories are also subject to narrative traditions, to selective traumatic amnesia, or to the directive manipulation of interviewers.

A recent Holocaust documentary, Yael Hersonski's production *A Film Unfinished*, released in 2010, is an attempt to deconstruct the Nazi project to document their atrocities for ideological purposes. The Third Reich Ministry of Propaganda produced several so called documentary films as part of their meticulously staged strategy of deception, such as *Der Führer schenkt den Juden eine Stadt* (The Führer Gives a City to the Jews, from 1944), a film that was supposed to deceive the world public by staging "normalcy" in the concentration camp Theresienstadt (Terezin).[9] In his film, Hersonski shows the filmic

---

[8] See Fred Camper, "*Shoah*'s Absence," in: Liebman, 103-111. The film "is haunted by those images we never see" (103).

[9] See Lutz Becker, "Film Documents of Theresienstadt," in: Haggith, 93-101.

material the Nazis produced depicting the Warsaw Ghetto to which he adds a critical commentary. This commentary is multi-layered and multi-faceted because it contains a narrating voice-over explaining the original production of the Nazi film, the selective construction of that film's reality, and the historical facts the film excludes. In addition, *A Film Unfinished* presents the testimonies of those who recorded the footage and those being depicted in the film in two ways: by reading documents written by the ghetto's inmates as well as the filming perpetrators and by having survivors watch scenes and comment on the Nazi material, thereby adding their personal experiences as a corrective insertion to the ideological narrative. The film's composition creates a complexity that pays tribute to the different perspectives and representations of and experiences embedded in the historic event. On one hand, *A Film Unfinished* delivers the most complete visual material of the living conditions in the ghetto and how these conditions were created through dehumanizing terror. On the other hand, the film reveals the construction of the Nazi's anti-Semitic propaganda film which stages "reality" in multiple takes, uses actors, and carefully follows a script. The Nazis present their cinematographic construction of reality to the viewing public as the "real," a juxtaposition of poverty and luxury in the ghetto as an expression of Jewish deception, or focusing on miserable conditions the Nazis themselves had created but now depicted as "natural" living conditions chosen by the Jewish ghetto population.

What makes this documentary somewhat problematic is the position of the camera when it records the survivor watching the footage of his/her own past. On the one hand, observing the survivor's reactions to what remains unseen turns the viewer into a voyeur par excellence, partaking in the survivor's pain of re-experiencing the events. On the other hand, the survivor is placed in a position of historical authority which is enhanced by the low angle of the camera. Following the self-reflexive commentary of the omnipotent narrator and the juxtaposition of two quoted witness accounts—the filmed victim and the filming perpetrator—the survivor has the last word as if he or she were the site of ultimate truth. The burden of such historical authority is unbearable, because it elevates the survivor above his/her fragile humanity, a humanity that always includes error, forgetting, or psychological breakdown vis-à-vis one's own trauma. What was evident already in Lanzmann's *Shoah* reoccurs in Hersonski's *A Film Unfinished*: the surviving witness cannot answer the fundamental questions regarding any logical reasoning underlying the event. Primo Levi's famous "here there is no why" echoes through all these interviews. The survivor does not allow for oversimplified identification when he or she refuses to give the interviewer the anticipated possibility of being the site for truth. Instead, the survivor might comment on the prosaic normality of being. For example, one witness exclaims, while watching the Nazi filmic material from the Warsaw Ghetto: "I might see my mother." As viewers we do not become witnesses "to the survivor's experience but [to] the making of testimony and its unique understanding of events" (Young 171).

Each of the documentaries discussed here exemplifies the multi-faceted challenges of representing the Holocaust as a historical event as well as an event of individual, personal trauma. These difficulties bring to the foreground the inability of the medium itself to portray complexities without reproducing the ideological framework of image-making and reducing the multitude of voices to a filmic meta-narrative that is subject to agency. While the image has limits when it comes to adequately representing violence and genocide, the compositional structure of these films questions whether we have yet to discover a postmodern redefinition of the genre "documentary" that takes into account the limitations of representational truth.

Works Cited

Adorno, Theodor W., "Kulturkritik und Geselllschaft." *Gesammelte Schriften*. Ed. Rolf Tiedemann. Darmstadt: Wissenschaftliche Buchgesellschaft, 1998. Vol. 10.1. 11-31.

Clendinnen, Inga. *Reading the Holocaust*. Cambridge: Cambridge University Press, 1999.

Ginsberg, Terri. *Holocaust Film: The Political Aesthetics of Ideology*. Newcastle: Cambridge Scholars Publishing, 2007.

Haggith, Toby, et. al., ed. Holocaust and the Moving Image: Representations in Film and Television Since 1933. London: Wallflower Press, 2005.

Insdorf, Annette. *Indelible Shadows: Film and the Holocaust*. 3rd Edition. Cambridge: Cambridge University Press, 2003.

Koch, Gertrud. Die Einstellung ist die Einstellung: visuelle Konstruktionen des Judentums. Frankfurt a. M.: Suhrkamp, 1992.

LaCapra, Dominick. *History and Memory after Auschwitz*. Ithaca: Cornell University Press, 1998.

Liebman, Stuart, ed. *Claude Lanzmann's SHOAH.* New York: Oxford University Press, 2007.

Rothberg, Michael. *Traumatic Realism. The Demands of Holocaust Representation.* Minneapolis: University of Minnesota Press, 2000.

Young, James. Writing and rewriting the Holocaust. Narrative and the Consequences of Interpretation. Bloomington: Indiana University Press, 1990.

Zelizer, Barbie, ed. *Visual Culture and the Holocaust.* New Brunswick; Rutgers University Press, 2000.

VIOLENCE, CONTINGENCE, ET INEGALITE SEXUELLE CHEZ MARYSE CONDE

Carine Mardorossian

Comment représenter la contingence de la violence sans pour autant remettre en question ou diminuer l'étendue et la sévérité de son impacte? Les approches postmodernes qui s'évertuent à démontrer et dissecter la contingence des mécanismes de pouvoir et d'oppression et qui insistent sur la relativité des opérations identitaires le font souvent au détriment de la réalité (si j'ose utiliser ce mot) de la violence qui est perpètuée contre les défavorisés sociaux. De fait, si les positions de pouvoir et d'inégalité ne sont plus perçues comme stables, la question de la sévérité de leur emprise devient d'autant plus pressante. Les problèmes d'inégalité sociale seraient-ils, dès lors, dus à des issues de représentation qui pourraient et devraient être changées? Ou sont-ils plutôt issues d'une domination qui précède la représentation qu'on s'en fait? Est-ce que le changement promu au niveau du langage pour effectuer des conditions plus démocratiques ne ferait pas partie d'une approche obfuscante qui réduit la réalité à sa représentation au lieu de l'affronter?

Cette communication examine la manière dont Maryse Condé souligne les dimensions contextualisantes des opérations de violence sans compromettre pour autant leurs effets sociaux traumatisants et endurants. Je propose de tracer les termes d'une telle éthique paradoxale dans un de ses romans, *Célanire Cou-coupé* spécifiquement, bien que, je maintiens, cette approache charactérise son corpus dans son entièreté. Et bien que l'oeuvre de Maryse Condé fournisse la base de ce travail, cette éthique créolisante mais incompromettante est commune à un bon nombre d'écrivaines contemporaines antillaises.

La contingence des structures d'oppression a été une des grandes révélations de la periode postmoderne, à tel point qu'elle adopte à présent une allure de banalité qui me fait prendre le risque d'avoir l'air bête en m'y arrêtant. Que quelqu'un dans une position subordonnée puisse jouer le rôle de l'oppresseur dans un autre contexte, va, nous l'espérons, de soi. De même, que la représentation de l'oppression et de la souffrance d'autrui a *en tant que* représentation des effets matériaux et idéologiques qui produisent la réalité même qui est censée être représentée est une autre réalisation qui semble entraîner un consensus critique aujourd'hui. Après Foucault, nous comprenons mieux comment il est possible qu'une représentation puisse précéder la réalité qu'on croyait être à l'origine de sa description. Et bien entendu, la question d'identité a aussi été délogée une fois pour toute du carcan essentialiste dans lequel elle avait été emprisonnée, puisqu'elle aussi est exposée comme le produit d'une construction plutôt que d'une condition naturelle qui précéderait sa représentation. Sans remettre en doute l'importance de l'intérêt que nous portons à la nature instable de toute transaction de pouvoir et d'identité, le problème avec ces épiphanies postmodernes contemporaines est qu'elles ont souvent lieu au détriment d'une vision politique progressiste qui s'empresserait de critiquer afin de la transformer la condition d'inégalité qui semblait nous préoccuper principalement dans un passé moins postmoderne. Il est plus difficile de s'insurger contre des injustices commises contre des identités et des personnes dont la nature est instable que de défendre des entités qui sont consistentes et fixes dans leur présence existentielle. Le fait que nous avons affaire à des constructions plutôt qu'à des vérités intelligibles et persistantes semble avoir freiné les résolutions émancipatrices de bon nombres d'écrivains et de voix critiques. Au lieu de condamnations des injustices et conflits sociaux représentés, on révèle l'impossibilité de déterminer la source du problème qui se fragmente dès lors sous nos yeux mêmes. La nature idéologique et donc changeante des relations sociales, sexuelles ou raciales semble dès lors couper l'herbe sous nos pieds critiques et nous nous trouvons en proie à la contingence de la violence.

En réponse à ce paradoxe de la critique contemporaine qui se veut interventioniste mais qui manque de fondation pour le devenir, un des gurus du postmodernisme contemporain, Judith Butler, s'est sentie obligée, dans l'introduction de son livre *Bodies that Matter*, de souligner que c'est une erreur de penser que le fait que les identités soient des constructions veut dire qu'elles sont dispensables: "[W]hy is it that what is constructed is understood as an artificial and dispensable character? What are we to make of constructions without which we would not be able to think, to live, to make sense at all, those which have acquired for us a kind of necessity" (v). On sent dans ce passage la frustration d'une philosophe dont les écrits ont été appropriés à des fins (a)politiques qui manquent de reflexivité envers les conséquences idéologiques, politiques, et matérielles de la pensée théorique.

Dans *Célanire cou-Coupé*, l'étonnant personnage de Célanire Pinceau souligne de manière fantastique et même monstrueuse le même principe que soulève Butler. Avec la force et la cruauté qui hantent son œuvre, Maryse Condé met en scène dans ce roman le supplice des peuples opprimés, et plus particulièrement celui des femmes martyrisées. Elle montre aussi, paradoxalement, comment les femmes elles-mêmes font souvent partie du mécanisme d'oppression qui les harcèle. L'histoire démarre au début du vingtième siècle avec l'arrivée du personnage central en Afrique pendant la période de l'avancée de la colonisation de l'Afrique par la France. En tant que missionaire, Célanire se fait remarquer en expérimentant une gestion différente du foyer dont elle devient directrice, féministe et progressiste, elle prend le parti des femmes battues et prône les recrutements de femmes et la libération des mœurs en Afrique. Anti-colonialiste, elle œuvre pour une vraie éducation des femmes et des hommes; elle défend l'idée que c'est en faisant prendre conscience aux africains de leurs capacités que l'on peut sortir l'Afrique de la colonisation.

D'un autre côté, si elle influe considérablement sur la gestion du Foyer des Métis, c'est grâce à ses liens privilégiés avec le gouverneur et une association plutôt problématique avec la présence coloniale. Elle est décrite comme diabolique, manipulatrice et implacable dans sa revanche, et le lecteur se pose la question de savoir si son empire féministe n'est pas en fait une façade pour une maison close par exemple. Le personnage devient un mélange de femme libre, épanouie, cosmopolitaine, peu préoccupée par les convenances, une femme qui vient de Guadeloupe mais voyage à travers l'Europe, l'Afrique, les Caraïbes et l'Amérique. Sa blessure abominable qui ressemble à un "sexe fendu" (Condé, *Célanire* 130) devient le symbole de la différence sexuelle qui définit l'héroïne ainsi que le monde d'inégalité dans lequel elle évolue.

Ce qui est remarquable dans le roman, c'est que le paradis féministe que Célanire met sur pied n'est pas un symbole unidimensionnel d'émancipation. Quand elle abrite la concubine du vieil oncle maternel du roi, l'adolescente Tanella qui avait tué le vieillard plutôt que de se livrer à ses fantasies, Célanire devient le site d'une impasse idéologique qui rappelle les écrits de Gayatri Spivak sur l'immolation par le feu des veuves en Inde. De fait, l'énoncé-choc de Spivak dans son essai important "Can the Subaltern Speak?" exprime la problématique de la position des femmes indiennes prises au piège entre la construction britannique du *suttee*, immolation par le feu linguistiquement réduite par les colonisateurs à une sublimation de leur rôle d'épouse, et la revendication autochtone de ce geste comme un acte autonome et un sacrifice délibéré. En d'autres termes, si la veuve se sacrifie, elle est victime du patriarcat indien et si elle refuse de se sacrifier, elle devient outil du colonialisme britannique qui se parade comme libérateur de la femme indienne pour justifier sa présence colonisatrice. *White men saving brown women from brown men.* En l'absence de la voix des femmes elles-mêmes, ces deux arguments se justifient mutuellement. Spivak remet en question la possibilité pour les colonisés de s'exprimer d'une seule voix dans une situation fracturée par le *suttee.* Une communauté hétérogène ne peut pas être identifiée à un seul point de vue et, si elle ne peut parler d'une seule voix qu'en réduisant au silence une partie de la communauté, elle ne peut pas non plus être représentée par les intellectuels post-coloniaux qui se posent en défenseurs des subalternes.

De même, dans *Célanire*, la réaction de la foule face à l'assassinat de Mawourou, l'oncle du roi Africain, révèle le même genre d'impasse subalterne. "En vérité, dans la foule, beaucoup de gens ne désiraient pas vraiment mettre Tanella à mort comme l'exigeait son crime. Ils marchaient avec les autres pour signifier tout simplement qu'il était temps, grand temps que ces Francais et leurs créatures, gouverneurs, prêtres, oblats les laissent à leurs coutumes et retournent chez eux. Même les femmes, qui, dans le fond de leur coeur, n'étaient pas loin d'excuser Tanella, sans doute fatiguée, nuit après nuit de livrer sa jeunesse aux fantaisies d'un vieillard, sentaient qu'avec ses ombres le passé qui agonisait l'emportait sur l'avenir que ces étrangers leur préparaient" (48). La foule se voit piégée par un choix qui n'en est pas vraiment un puisqu'il lui a été imposé par l'histoire et les moeurs sociaux: celui entre le colonialisme qui définit "ces étrangers" et le patriarcat qui oppresse les femmes du pays et que l'on défend à cause du contexte colonial qu'il oppose. Ce passage révèle à quel point la femme indigène devient un site à travers lequel divergentes idéologies se rencontrent, s'entrechoquent, et prennent le dessus sans tenir compte de ses droits, besoins, ou désirs.

De même, Célanire, malgré son adhérence à des principes anti-colonialistes *et* féministes voit ces deux principes en contradiction l'un avec l'autre quand pour défendre Tanella, elle a recours aux miliciens du gouverneur qui finissent par tuer deux gamins d'une dizaine d'années. Les deux enfants s'avèrent être les fils du roi Koffi Ndizi ce qui illustre d'autant plus explicitement comment ses positions féministes sont incommensurables avec des attitudes anticolonialistes. En restant fidèle à ses principes féministes, elle cause la mort de deux innocents qui, par leur relation filiale, représentent la culture traditionnelle. Le même paradoxe définit la décision de l'héroïne de créer un Musée ethnographique d'Afrique Noire, pour montrer "aux orphelins du Foyer mais aussi à ceux qui en douteraient que L'Afrique possède sa propre culture. Masques dan, wobe, gouro, yaoure, baoule, mais surtout *guere*, les maîtres du genre. Les plus belle pièces du musée étaient une série de neuf masques *guere*: un masque chanteur, deux masques guerriers, danseurs, un masque de la sagesse, un masque de course, un masque de comédie, un masque griot ... Célanire n'hésitait pas à approcher les chefs, les anciens, à se mêler à des sociétés secrètes ou à des cérémonies d'initiation. Cela choquait profondèment les Africains qui se plaignirent qu'elle pillait leur patrimoine sacré... Les femmes ne doivent pas regarder les masques, à plus forte raison leur mettre la main dessus: à cause de cela, elle n'enfanterait jamais. Ni garçon, ni fille." (125-6). Les actions de l'héroïne qui sont censées reconnaître l'autorité culturelle du patrimoine africain sont au contraire reçues comme une extension d'attitudes colonisantes. Nous nous trouvons donc sans cesse dans des situations où des démarches progressistes sont perçues comme oppressives ou ont des effets opprimants, alors que la domination coloniale qui produit et dépend de ce genre d'impasse n'est pas remise en question.

Ces descriptions insistent donc sur la contingence des opérations de pouvoir et d'oppression, de résistance et de rébellion, mais sans remettre en doute la culpabilité d'un système qui crée des impasses idéologiques et politiques comme celles que je viens de décrire. Dans *Écrire en Pays Dominé*, Patrick Chamoiseau explique qu'un des symptômes de la vie dans un monde dominé est que le pouvoir ne fonctionne plus par imposition mais par obfuscation. Nous vivons, nous dit-il, dans une ère de domination que nous ne pouvons plus voir. C'est ce mode de fonctionnement d'un pouvoir qui obscurcit que Condé représente dans sa fiction, un pouvoir qui tourne le combat féministe en complice du colonialisme et compromet les interventions anti-colonialistes de Célanire. Ces dynamiques établissent des tensions insurmontables entre les divers mouvements progressistes qui essaient de se soustraire au carcan colonialiste ou patriarcal et désamorcent toute intervention individualiste.

La théorisation d'identité que nous offre Condé à travers son corpus littéraire expose une impasse similaire quant il en vient à la découverte d'alternatives plausibles aux dichotomies raciales. Condé s'est depuis ses tout premiers romans penchée sur la question de la race comme d'un fléau qui divise l'humanité au nom d'une catégorie qui est aussi arbitraire qu'elle est tenace. Se faisant l'écho de Glissant, Condé nous montre que le métissage et l'hybridité qui sont conçus comme un croisement entre une race blanche et une race noire pour aboutir à un mélange "café au lait" (*Célanire* 30) n'échappe pas à la logique raciale que l'écrivaine attaque dans ses romans. Dans *Célanire Cou-Coupé*, par exemple, Condé évoque la couleur qu'on associe avec le croisement racial quand elle réfère à "une peau variant du brun jaunâtre jusqu'au blanc cassé" (86), la peau "café au lait" (30), pour parler des enfants qui vivent au Foyer des Métis. Le Foyer, c'est aussi l'endroit où l'amour interracial est supposé proliférer et nous débarrasser des divisions raciales et nationales. Il est évident pour Condé que cette vision utopique est absurde et ne menace pas "l'épistémologie de visibilité" (Wiegman 4) qui définit le racisme, c'est-à-dire cette manière qu'il a d'associer les races à des signes corporels visibles. C'est la même épistémologie de visibilité que Condé met en relief dans *Histoire de la Femme Cannibale*, quand le narrateur s'exclame qu'il est "entendu que ceux de l'ethnie de Deogratias, les 'descendants des pasteurs,' ne sont pas vraiment des Nègres. Regardez leur stature, leur sveltesse! Voyez surtout leur nez aquilin! Un nez, cela veut tout dire!" (47). Cette remarque fait bien entendu référence aux discours pseudo-scientifiques du 19ème siècle pour qui la race est déterminée par des descriptions corporelles comme par exemple la taille du nez, des yeux, la couleur des yeux, la taille du pénis ou de la poitrine pour les femmes. C'est un discours naturalisant du corps human, un des deux "fléaux qui interdisent la communication entre hommes" (178). C'est aussi le produit d'une épistémologie de visibilité qui fait appel à des différences soit-disant biologiques et incontournables mais--Maryse Condé nous montre d'une manière très convaincante et nuancée roman après roman – qui est en fait produit par un système de croisement identitaire qui va tellement de soi aujourd'hui qu'il faut vraiment s'appliquer pour l'identifier. Ce croisement n'est pas un simple fait de métissage puisqu'il implique plus d'une seule catégorie d'identité et dépend de l'intersection de la race avec d'autres catégories identitaires comme la différence sexuelle, la nationalité, la sexualité, etc. C'est une forme d'hybridité qui ne s'arrête donc pas à l'intersection de races entre elles mais tient compte de la façon dont le sens acquis par le concept de race est stabilisé grâce à son association avec d'autres catégories identitaires.

Dans *Histoire de la Femme Cannibale*, le "couple domino" (52) Rosélie (l'héroïne Guadeloupéene) et Stephen (l'Européen blanc) perpétuent à travers leur relation interraciale les paramètres les plus racistes de leur société (il parle de la femme noire comme "l'inconnue, la source d'un mystère, comme vulnérable et perdue" (30). Elle se définit comme une impuissante victime (206)). En fait, Condé nous dit dans son style polémique typique que "l'adage que l'on croit à tort raciste est véridique: 'Tous les Noirs se ressemblent'" (202). Qu'est-ce qu'elle peut bien entendre par là? Elle a des personnages noirs qui se comportent de manière complètement stéréotypée, de manière extrêmement sexuelle par exemple et dont les membres sexuels sont décrits comme prononcés, etc. Alors comment parvient-elle à montrer qu'il n'y a de fait pas de "races, que des cultures" (notes 14) si ces représentations semblent reproduire de tels stéréotypes raciaux?

Condé, je maintiens, ne veut pas contredire les stéréotypes parce que les rejeter explicitement est une manière de leur octroyer une autorité qu'elle ne veut pas risquer de leur donner. Ce qu'elle fait donc au lieu de les contester, c'est de remplacer le modèle de lecture qui consiste à déterminer si un personnage est noir, blanc ou métisse avant d'examiner leur rôle dans le récit par un modèle qui souligne la manière dont la race d'un individu change et se développe d'après les contextes (narratifs ou culturels) dans lesquels il ou elle se trouve. C'est dans le contexte de leur comportement non-conformiste pas exemple que leur différence raciale prend une nouvelle envergure dans le récit. Cette représentation nous encourage à voir l'identité non pas comme un attribut fixe mais comme un narratif qui se développe et change d'après les actions des personnages.

Les romans de l'écrivaine Guadeloupéenne révèlent qu'il est impossible d'analyser le problème de la race (ou de l'identité sexuelle) sans tenir compte de la manière dont chaque catégorie, loin d'être préexistante et stable, est produite par son articulation avec d'autres concepts. En d'autres termes, c'est à travers son articulation plutôt que dans sa singularité ou isolation que chaque identité obtient son sens et est associée à une série de traits *a posteriori*. C'est quand le personnage croise et transgresse une limite identitaire que ce croisement est naturalisé par un recours à un autre site de croisement identitaire. Par exemple, quand le personnage transgresse les conventions sexuelles, elle est identifiée comme "noire" ou quand il s'engage dans une relation interraciale qui menace le status quo, il devient féminisé. C'est à cause de ce système de doubles croisements identitaires que Rosélie dans *Histoire de la Femme Cannibale* est coincée entre une politique d'exclusion ou d'invisibilité: "Triste choix! Exclusion ou invisibilité!" (47). Quand elle est la compagne d'un homme blanc, elle est visible, et quand elle est veuve, elle devient invisible. Même l'épistémologie de visibilité fonctionne d'une manière contingente puisqu'elle ne devient apparente que d'après le contexte dans lequel le personnage évolue.

Le mari de Rosélie, à cause de sa liaison interraciale évoque tout de suite la suspicion de la présence de miscégénation dans la famille "Stephen Stewart, n'était pas un natif-natal. Son père était un Anglais du Royaume-Uni.... Sa mère française l'avait élevé du côté de Verberie, dans l'Oise. D'une certaine manière, cette facette de son hérédité expliquait l'outrage! Les Francais ont des goûts impurs, car ils ont le sang impur et sont plus qu'à moitié métèques. Des peuples de tous acabits ont enjambé les frontières de l'Hexagone, campé et fait leur couche en son mitan" (19). Ce passage démontre bien l'impossibilité de conceptualiser un croisement identitaire sans avoir recours à une autre catégorie d'identité: la relation interraciale de Stephen est une transgression raciale qui tout de suite soulève la question d'autres transgressions sexuelles dans la famille. Une forme de croisement est configurée par son association avec une autre. Dans *Célanire cou-coupé*, ce mécanisme est encore plus évident puisque l'héroïne transcende les limites identitaires de tous côtés: elle devient animale, métisse, noire-noire, lesbienne, masculine, ultra-féminine, hétérosexuelle d'après ses transgressions sociales, sexuelles, ou morales.

Dès le début du récit, Célanire est décrite en termes animaliers avec ses "jolies dents carnassières" (20) et sa "grosse natte noire, qu'on aurait dit dotée d'une vie autonome, [et qui] serpentait le long de son dos" (87). Nous apprenons que sa résurrection eut lieu grâce à une infusion de sang de poulet, et elle est constamment comparée à des animaux prédateurs (araignée carnivore, chat, python, etc.). Ces références récurrentes exposent le processus idéologique à travers lequel l'alterité raciale ou sexuelle est produite non pas par des différences naturalisantes mais par son association avec des tropes comme l'animalité, la saleté, la contagion, etc. C'est parce que Célanire est un personnage dont la différence est si intractable et instable que les autres personnages s'évertuent à la fixer en ayant recours à de telles associations. De fait, il est important de noter que la caractérisation de Célanire ne nous est accessible qu'à travers les perspectives focalisantes des gens qu'elle rencontre: Karamanlis le Grec, Hakim le musulman, Thomas de Brabant le nouveau gouverneur, sa femme

Charlotte, la fille de Charlotte Ludivine, le père adoptif de Célanire (Pinceau), etc. Ces personnages ont sans cesse recours à des stéréotypes pour parler de Célanire parce qu'ils ne parviennent pas à "contenir" ce "sexe fendu" (130).

De plus, parce que le narrateur adopte un détachement complet vis-à-vis du discours stéréotypé des personnages, il est d'autant plus difficile pour le lecteur de discerner un jugement sur la manière dont les conceptions les plus outrageantes au sujet de Célanire sont produites. La distinction entre la façon dont Célanire est perçue et qui elle est devient d'autant plus difficile à determiner vu l'ironie voilée du narrateur combiné avec un style indirect de narration. Quand les personnnages mâles font constamment référence à l'ensorcellement auquel Célanire les soumet, cela peut-être aussi bien une fonction du comportement de l'héroïne dans le récit que des clichés à travers lesquels elle est perçue à cause de nonconformisme. Par exemple, il n'est pas clair si Célanire est de fait la compagne de Tanelle ou si c'est sa violation des normes féminines qui font que les personnages la perçoivent comme une lesbienne. Le lecteur attentif se pose la question, et celui qui l'est moins risque par contre de reproduire les pensées généralisantes qui lui sont offertes par la focalisation sans se poser de questions. Sans nous guider, Condé nous laisse décider.

De même, les transmogrifications cannibales de Célanire en chien sauvage, cheval, et autres animaux sont une manière littérale pour le récit de commenter sur le processus d'interpellation raciale. Le vocabulaire utilisé pour décrire la différence raciale de Célanire dépend de son association avec l'animalité et l'excès, mais il est rendu instable par le récit fantastique dans lequel elle évolue. Le roman met sur pied le mécanisme symbolique grâce auquel les identités sont produites et normalisées, mais le déstabilise en même temps vu son recours au fantastique. Il introduit sans arrêt une fissure entre la matérialité du corps et les traits qui le produisent comme base fixe et essentielle de l'identité parce que le processus d'association qui est à la base de cette production est révélé comme arbitraire. Quand nous rencontrons Célanire à Adjame-Santey où contrairement à son séjour à Lyon, nous nous attendrions à ce que la couleur de sa peau ne la signale plus "partout comme un flambeau" (19), les gens continuent à tourner la tête parce que "sa couleur la mettait à part, cette peau noire qui l'habillait comme un vêtement de grand deuil" (14). Sa différence raciale est configurée par son association avec la compétence linguistique: "ils tournaient la tête et essayaient de distinguer les traits de cette créature surprenante, noire de peau, mais parlant la langue des Blancs, vivant avec eux, habillée comme eux" (19). Cette description révèle de nouveau la fissure qui sépare l'identité raciale de la différence corporelle qui soi-disant la définit. L'identité raciale de Célanire change donc d'après les transgressions de normes sexuelles de l'héroïne "qui n'[est] pas ordinaire" (14).

Cette représentation expose la manière dont les sites d'identité performent des opérations complexes et symboliques afin de créer l'apparence d'une stabilité que nous avons normalisée au dépend des associations arbitraires qui la rendent possible. Ces associations sont le résultat de croisements identitaires à travers lesquels une transgression de normes est configurée par son association avec un autre croisement identitaire. Cette forme d'hybridité est donc loin d'être subversive puisqu'elle permet au discours dominant de contenir les transgressions des personnages plutôt que de mener à un discours alternatif qui remettrait la norme en question. C'est précisément parce que les récits de Condé refusent de célébrer cette hybridité interidentitaire à tout prix qu'ils ne tombent pas dans le piège du postmodernisme. Au contraire, ils démontrent que la contigence qui définit nos identités ne les libère pas pour autant du carcan essentialiste dans le contexte duquel la question de l'identité est normalement envisagée. Certes, c'est au nom d'identités fixes et de différences catégoriques que la violence sociale est perpetuée, mais c'est l'appropriation d'un régime de croisements contingents qui rend cette production de normes possible. Les romans de Condé nous démontrent comment les identités qui nous sont si chères quand il en vient à définir l'être humain sont des récits que nous avons naturalisés bien qu'ils soient littéralement construits de toutes pièces. C'est l'articulation de nos différences avec d'autres catégories qui déterminent leurs sens. Ce que les représentations "fantastiques" de Condé exposent donc de manière si intransigeante, c'est que les identités soi-disant discrètes au nom desquelles la violence est pérpetuée n'en sont pas moins violentes pour être basées sur une dynamique d'hybridité contingente. Certes, la différence sexuelle ou raciale sont des produits du language plutôt que d'une différence biologique, et c'est important de noter la nature symbolique de l'identité. Mais Condé nous démontre en même temps que la contingence que nous exposons si fièrement par nos interventions critiques est moins une conséquence non désirée des opérations de pouvoir (qui, exposée, l'affaiblirait) que la base même de son fonctionnement.

Bibliographie

Abramson, Julia. "Review of *Célanire Cou-Coupé*." *World Literature To-day* 75.2 (Spring 2001): 306.

Butler, Judith. *Bodies that Matter: On the Discursive Limits of "Sex."* New York: Routledge, 1993.

Chamoiseau, Patrick. *Écrire en Pays Dominé.* Paris: Gallimard, 1997.

Condé, Maryse. Célanire Cou-Coupé. Paris: Robert Laffont, 2000.

---. *Histoire de La Femme Cannibale.* Paris: Mercure de France, 2003.

---. "Notes sur un Retour au Pays Natal." *Conjunction: Revue Franco-Haïtienne* 176 (Supplément 1987): 7-23.

Foucault, Michel. *Histoire de la sexualité.* Vol. 1. Paris: Gallimard, 1976.

Glissant, Édouard. *Poétique de la Relation.* Paris: Gallimard, 1990.

Spivak, Gayatri Chakravorty. "Can the Subaltern Speak? Speculations on Widow Sacrifice." *Marxism and the Interpretation of Culture.* Eds. Cary Nelson and Lawrence Grossberg. London: Macmillan, 1988. 271-313.

Wiegman, Robyn. *American Anatomies: Theorizing Race and Gender.* Durham: Duke UP, 1995.

MEDITERRANEAN AND FRENCH CARIBBEAN PAROXYSMS: MARIE FERRANTI'S VIOLENT DISCOURSE ABUT CORSICA

Silvia Baage

> L'histoire a des exigences de précision
> que le roman peut éluder [...].
> Marie Ferranti, *Une haine de Corse*, 2012.

Scholars, critics, and essayists like Édouard Glissant, Antonio Benítez-Rojo, and Daniel Maximin have already produced countless critical works to explain the unrepresentability of the French Caribbean contemporary imaginary and its radical techniques of resistance to French assimilation.[1] Corsican forms of cultural expression in French, however, have undoubtedly received less attention. In particular, Corsican scholars Anne Meistersheim and Jean-Louis Andreani take issue with the problematic relationship between Corsica and Metropolitan France. While Corsica's geographic situation as Europe's most mountainous island is oftentimes compared to Indian and Pacific Ocean islands, little research has been done on the Corsican side to further explore what Daniel Maximin calls the geopoetics of violence.[2]

In their analysis of French Caribbean specificities, Édouard Glissant, Chris Bongie, and Daniel Maximin use the example of Corsican difference as a strategic counterpoint. While Glissant compares the concept of diffraction for the French Caribbean to the concept of refraction for the Mediterranean to describe two different visions of islandedness,[3] Maximin argues that both regions share symmet-

---

[1] See Benítez, Rojo A. The Repeating Island: The Caribbean and the Postmodern Perspective. Durham: Duke University Press, 1992; Glissant, Édouard. Discours antillais. Paris: Gallimard, 2007 ; Maximin, Daniel. Les Fruits du cyclone: une géopoétique de la Caraïbe. Paris: Seuil, 2006.

[2] Several contributions to *Ces Îles où l'on parle français* (Paris: Hérodote, 1985) specifically engage with this point.

[3] "The Caribbean Sea diffracts right where we would consider, for example, that the sea can also have a civilizing effect; at first, the Mediterranean Sea

rical patterns of violence. This symmetry leads Maximin to view the French Caribbean as a local mirror image of the Mediterranean, or "American Mediterranean." This paper will contribute to on-going discussions in Francophone Studies about marginalized regions of the French-speaking world by exploring these frequently overlooked communalities and disjunctions that govern the histories of violence and difference in Corsica and the French Caribbean. I will first focus on the representation of the experience of taking root on these is-lands, and then move on to the relationship between tropical island nature and violent histories and cultures. The last section of this pa-per will be devoted to a brief analysis of these concepts in a contem porary Corsican novel, *La Fuite aux Agriates* (Gallimard, 2000), writ-ten by Marie Ferranti.

1. The French Caribbean and Corsican experience

Daniel Maximin is a Guadeloupean author, poet, and critic. In his 2006 essay, *Les Fruits du cyclone: une géopoétique de la Caraïbe,* Maximin highlights three important aspects of discourses that show traces of how to overcome a difficult past. First of all, he reiterates Glissant's notion of *drifting islands [la dérive]* that ideologically speaking exist in and by themselves: "Caribbean cultures are therefore characterized by the complete rejection of encirclement, aesthetic or ideological injunction other than the claim for freedom. Against the prisons of styles, languages, genres, manifestos of literature, plastic arts, or mu-sic. And victory of the gravity of resentments" [« Les cultures cari-béennes se caractérisent ainsi par le refus total de tout encerclement, de tout injonction esthétique ou idéologique, autre que l'exigence de liberté. Contre les prisons des styles, des langues, des genres, des ma-nifestes littéraires, plastiques ou musicaux. Et de la victoire sur la pesanteur des ressentiments »] (Maximin 17). Maximin situates the region's vigorous attempts to express its specificities and claims for autonomy within the historical context of political and economic inequalities. He draws on the antithetical nature of certainty and doubt as foundational building blocks of a new form of cultural ex-

---

had a power of attraction and concentration" [« La mer Caraïbe diffracte, là où par exemple on estimera qu'une mer elle est aussi civilisatrice, la Médi-terranée, avait d'abord puissance d'attraction et de concentration » (*Discours* 729). All translations are my own and they are as literal as possible.

pression that reverses oppression and diverts from French assimilation:

> "[...] one can easily measure the weakness of such as birth initiated during four centuries of oppression, locked into the narrow passageway of a geography of island isolation, with the temptation to sometimes alienate from one, sometimes other imposed European debris of lost Africa, and the creation of a culture based on alternating doubt and confidence, hope and despise: *mystery from the seas!*"

> [« [...] on peut mesurer sans peine la fragilité d'une telle genèse initiée en quatre siècle d'opression, enfermée dans l'étroit passage d'une géographie d'isolement insulaire, avec la tentation de s'aliéner tantôt à l'un, tantôt à l'autre des débris d'Europe imposée ou d'Afrique perdue, et l'édification d'une culture bâtie sur l'alternance du doute et de la confiance, de l'espoir et du mépris: *énigme parmi les eaux !* »] (215).

As this passage indicates, the marginalized and oppressed islanders managed to overcome the cumulative effects of forced alienation from an incompatible present and their lost ties to the past. For Maximin, the experience of alienation and the somewhat belated determination to finally build a new culture from remaining fragments are fundamental steps towards the act of "constructing a form of dignity" ["se bâtir une dignité"] (216-217).

As a second characteristic, Maximin insists on the fact that although uncertainty and disdain will remain inherent parts of this constructive experience, they are effectively counter-balanced by a more positive, self-assertive attitude. This approach towards a newly reborn culture facilitates the transformation of the French Caribbean's status from mere transitional space (*lieu de passage*) into a solid space where roots are taken (*terre d'enracinement*):

> [...] paradoxically, the French Caribbean islands have the ambiguous status of being **deserted islands** that are too narrow to take roots, and of being **treasure islands** that are receptacles of the most extreme forms of greed. As **transitional islands**, they were able to transform themselves into **islands of refuge** for those who did not have any hope of returning to their continent, that is, deported Africans, in a space of reception for the exiled, their resistance, and their revival. Those who did not expect anything, on the ground

of the ship's hold, were able to take roots here and to find the energy to re-create. This is the difference between the African voyage and the European voyage [...] All African Robinsons became Fridays, while Daniel Defoe's Robinson did nothing but prepare his return that left him richer with everything he had taken and everything he had learned. The last one who was forced to come decides that he is at home.

[...] paradoxalement, les îles caraïbes ont eu un statut ambigu d'**îles désertes** trop étroites pour les enracinements, et d'**îles aux trésors réceptacles** des plus extrêmes cupidités. **Iles de passage**, elles ont pu se transformer en **îles refuges** d'abord pour ceux qui n'avaient aucun espoir de retour sur leur continent, c'est-à-dire les Africains déportés, en un espace d'accueil pour leur exil, leur résistance et leur renaissance. Ceux qui n'attendaient rien, au fond de la cale, ont pu s'y enraciner et y trouver les forces de la re-création. Là est la différence entre le voyage africain et le voyage européen [...] Tous les Robinsons africains sont devenus des Vendredis, tandis que le Robinson de Daniel de Foë ne préparait que son retour, qu'il effectuera plus riche de tout ce qu'il aura pris et appris. Le dernier arrivé de force décide qu'il est chez lui (84-85 ; my emphasis added in bold).

The descriptive words that qualify the status of the island illustrate the extraordinary metamorphosis of a piece of land surrounded on all sides by water that basically transforms from being nothing but a deserted island to being a treasure island before eventually becoming a refuge and home, where African Robinsons become Fridays. But can these French Caribbean Fridays accumulate wealth?

According to Maximin, the last characteristic inherent to the French Caribbean experience is the act of taking root. This characteristic becomes a particularly relevant paradigm for Maximin to consider the reconfiguration of French Caribbean socio-political and cultural epistemologies. While dispersed fragments are commonly found in a *lieu de passage,* in a *terre d'enracinement,* these dispersed pieces of debris are salvaged to form new, somewhat more meaningful units that Glissant described as the poetics of Relation. Maximin suggests that "Everything that has been lost, stolen, forgotten, rejected, has secretly been reincarnated into a *poetics of the relation,* the way Glissant defined it, between human slaves and the island accomplice" ["Tout ce qui avait été perdu, volé, violé, oublié, renié, a pu se réincarner secrètement dans une *poétique de la relation*, comme la définit Glissant, entre l'homme esclave et l'île complice]" (81-82). But Maximin underscores the creative use of seemingly rejected fragments or debris: "The Caribbean invents for itself a human form [...] on the grounds of the colored snippets it [...] grazes from nature so much as humans. It's a fiddler of nests [...] the building of our peoples with the *debris of synthesis:* gleaned fetuses, pieces of stolen string, trimming, recuperated leftovers" [« la Caraïbe s'invente une forme humaine [...] à partir des bribes colorées qu'[elle] picore tant dans la nature que chez les humains. C'est un bricoleur de nid [... il s'agit d'une] édification de nos peuples avec des *débris de synthèses* : fétus glanés, bouts de ficelle volés, rognures, restes récupérés »] (21-22). Although gleaning leftovers becomes an extremely creative alternative to assimilation that facilitates the negotiation of a long and difficult history of oppression and inequalities, it has led critics to draw different conclusions about the way islanders manage their islandedness. This takes us back to the idea of the island as being surrounded by an ocean that either diffracts or refracts the space of the island.

On the Mediterranean island of Corsica, the acts of doubting, transitioning, and assembling debris take on a particular function. Contrary to the sugar cane plantation economy system of the French Caribbean that heavily relied on the labor of imported slaves, Corsica was converted into a colony early on by the Romans and the Greeks for strategic purposes. The island saw numerous devastating battles that translate the desperate attempts of successive rulers such as Genoa and Piza who tried to gain control. These tensions regularly opposed outside powers and the inhabitants of Corsica. But compared to their French Caribbean counterparts, Corsicans have, as Janine Renucci indicates, a remarkable history of resistance that forms the foundation of what is known today as the Corsican insular identity that foregrounds a right to be different. This insularity (rather than islandedness) fundamentally relies on activities from the underground.

The Corsican author, critic, and journalist Jean-Louis Andreani brings up this very point when describing contemporary Corsica as an exploited French colony, from the Genoa era to the present:

> With regard to Corsica's situation at the end of the 20th century, the reference to colonialism can seem anachronistic or irrelevant. But it is not tacked from nowhere on to reality of

the island's past. During the entire Genoa era, the island experienced a colonial situation, in the strict sense of the meaning: exploitation of natural resources for the exclusive benefit of the metropolitan center, discrimination and bullying of the native population. France herself continued until the 20ᵗʰ century to tax exportations of island productions that were coming to the continent, which is an unquestionable sign of an unequal relationship.

[À propos de la Corse de la fin du XXᵉ siècle, la référence au fait colonial peut paraître anachronique ou hors de propos. Mais elle n'est pas plaquée de l'extérieur sur la réalité du passé insulaire. Pendant toute l'époque génoise, l'île a vécu une situation coloniale, au sens strict du terme : exploitation des ressources naturelles au profit exclusif de la métropole, discrimination et brimades à l'égard des autochtones. La France elle-même continuera jusqu'au début du XXᵉ siècle à taxer l'exportation de productions insulaires à destination du continent, signe incontestable d'une relation inégalitaire (161)].

Exploiting the island's resources, discriminating, bullying, and imposing taxes on exports to continental France are common occurrences, despite the fact that both *Haute-Corse* and *Corse-du-Sud* are two of France's 101 administrative departments out of which five are located overseas (four of them being islands). An island of France, Corsica is actually composed of a blend of Mediterranean cultures and civilizations that landed on the island, similar to the way the islands in the French Caribbean were populated by four different continents. The next section will focus on the impact of geography and climate in its relationship to the history and culture of these blends of different populations on the island.

2. Patterns of violence: climate, nature, and society

Numerous French writers and thinkers including Jean-Jacques Rousseau and Madame de Staël have theorized about the impact of climatic differences on human conduct, from the Middle Ages to the Romantic period and beyond. These theories started taking political tones to describe the complexity of encounters between two types of temperaments in colonial and postcolonial contexts, as Chris Bongie indicates.[4] Authors and filmmakers from French-speaking Africa have dealt with the topic of violence in various ways but within the context of this study, it seems particularly enriching to return to Daniel Maximin's essay as the author specifically examines the connection between the relationship of history and nature in the Mediterranean and the French Caribbean.

Maximin's essay sets out to explain recurring patterns of violence by combining the analogy of rude temperaments of people living in hot countries on the one hand, and Camus's vision of violence in colonial contexts on the other hand. While Camus finds comfort in the soothing nature at dawn and dusk to recover from the insufferable heat during the day, Maximin posits that the tropical nature and climate of his archipelago is far away from providing calm and serenity to the distressed human observer:

> We can make a very productive comparison with the *Southern thought [pensée de midi]* of the Mediterranean that we find in this one sentence of Albert Camus that has long been engraved in my memory: **'Misery does not hinder the belief that everything under the son and in history is good; sun taught me that history is not good at all.'** This thought is very Mediterranean and comes from a space that is African, European, and also Oriental, with a powerful balance between the forces of nature in relationship to the temperate North and to the desert that serves as its border in the South, and that shares ties with the Caribbean, our American Mediterranean Sea. What is similar is that we are also a space where misery and sun attack. Nevertheless, Camus distinguished between two worlds that, according to him, were drastically different: violence is a part of history and nature counterbalances it as a sign of hope and craving for pleasure, exhaustion. But in the Caribbean, **calamities are also natural**.
>
> [On pourrait ici faire une comparaison toujours très fertile avec la *pensée de midi* de la Méditerranée, que l'on retrouve dans cette phrase d'Albert Camus depuis très longtemps gravée dans ma mémoire : **'La misère m'empêcha de croire que tout est bon sous le soleil et dans l'histoire ;**

---

[4] See Bongie, Chris. Islands and Exiles: The Creole Identities of Post/Colonial Literature. Stanford: Stanford University Press, 1998.

le soleil m'apprit que l'histoire n'est pas du tout'. Pensée très méditerranéenne, venue d'un lieu au monde à la fois
africain, européen, oriental, avec un puissant équilibre entre
les forces de la nature par rapport au Nord tempérée et au
désert qui le circonscrit au sud, et qui partage bien les cousi-
nages avec la Caraïbe, notre Méditerranée américaine. La
ressemblance, c'est que nous sommes aussi un lieu entre mi-
sère et soleil à leur paroxysme. Cependant, Camus oppose
deux mondes selon lui radicalement distincts : la violence est
dans l'histoire, et la nature vient de la contrebalancer, elle est
porteuse des espérances, des soifs de jouissance,
d'épanouissement. Or, dans la Caraïbe, **les cataclysmes
sont aussi naturels** (101; my emphasis added in bold)].

Maximin thus challenges Camus's theory of the balance between a calm, tropical nature to soothe the violent history of Corsica,
to consider the cumulative effects of the destructive forces of nature
and climate of the French Caribbean which are magnified by its violent history: "The islands fold up under the storms, drown under
tidal waves, break through earthquakes, and are burned by volcanos.
With a history that keeps imitating these four geographical calamities."
[« Iles pliées sous les ouragans, noyées sous les raz-de-marée, fractu-
rées par les séismes, grillées vives par leurs volcans. Avec une histoire
qui s'est acharnée à imiter en tout point ces quatre cataclysmes de la
géographie » (14)]. In other words, the destructive forces of violent
outbursts of nature other than the sun are an essential part of French
Caribbean everyday-life.

While Corsica does not have a direct equivalent to the destructive forces of French Caribbean nature, the island finds itself in another extreme situation that is directly related to its geographical situation rather than its climatic influences or its being exposed to natural catastrophes. Janine Renucci is not the only researcher to explain
the singular demographic distribution of Corsicans throughout its
mountainous surface. Jean-Louis Andreani emphasizes that the
combination of mountainous seclusion, in addition to the geographic
fact of being an island, reinforced the emergence of the Corsicans'

---

5 The last part of this sentence is probably mistyped and should read: "[…]
le soleil m'apprit que l'histoire ne l'est pas du tout."

perception of their difference, la *Corsitude.*[6] This difference encompasses two traditional systems of violence, with one being related to an internal system of island-specific honor codes, and the second being the violence of successive waves of invasion. The question then becomes how contemporary island discourses deal with these occurrences of violence in the historic past of the island and how do they appropriate them to what Maeve McCusker and Anthony Soares refer to as a "supposedly postcolonial context [where] islands offer perhaps the most potent, distressing, and anomalous images of the neocolonial project, and can thus be seen to exemplify the complex afterlives of empire" (xv).

When considering the commonalities and disjunctions between the French Caribbean and Corsica, it is important to take into consideration the aesthetic function of violence in French-speaking texts of both regions. In *Intention poétique,* Glissant pointed to the epistemological limits of Occidental realism to account for the excessive dimensions of French Caribbean discursive patterns "to **scream out** this singularity of the world and the human being" ["pour **crier** cet unique du monde et de l'être" (11; my emphasis added). Glissant specifically defines this scream as contradictory poetics that eventually transform into *une parole* or speech. This transformation from scream to *parole*[7] is further analyzed in the 1989 Creoleness manifesto,

---

[6] *Corsitude* is a particular behavior by which the islander makes it a point to consider his 'insularity' in the English sense of the term. While French critics use the term *insularité* to analyze what Corsican critics Jean-Louis Andreani and Anne Meistersheim refer to as the sociopolitical and economic consequences that come with the geographical fact of being an island, the immediate equivalent in the English language, *insularity,* has rather negative connotations of isolation and seclusion. These negative connotations, however, tend to be expressed by two separate words in French, *insularisme* and *iléité* that both play a major role in *Corsitude* (Meistersheim "Insularité").

[7] "And everywhere music made its way through silence to liberate **the scream** [...] Not to **scream,** but to **create** [...] And this transformation from **scream to song**, from chains to dance, the artist, the slave of the law of reality, improvises an art whose new aesthetics are to depict a possible form of hope by showing to the community through the example of aesthetic commitment that follows the example of the fugitive slave, that the possibility of emergence between doubt and faith, brings about nocturnal creations at the sound of the drum (41-42; my emphasis)." [« Et partout la musique a traversé le silence pour délivrer **le cri** [...] Non pour **crier**, mais pour **créer** [...] Et par **ce passage du cri au chant**, de la chaîne à la danse,

Eloge de la Créolité [In Praise of Creoleness], where Jean Bernabé, Patrick Chamoiseau, and Raphaël Confiant underlined the self-defining and affirmative qualities of the French Caribbean *cri d'appel* that, according to Maximin, has an organizational structure and rhythmical nature.

Although the theme of violence is heavily materialized in colonial and postcolonial representations of Corsica in the works of continental and island-based authors, they do not have the same poetic or even prophetic function as narrative event than those that are geared towards the French Caribbean. This specificity is particularly evident in Marie Ferranti's contemporary adaptation of Mérimée's 1840 short story "Carmen" in her 2000 novel, *La Fuite aux Agriates*, in which she depicts gendered violence and terror from a female perspective.

3. Narrating violence: A gendered perspective on violence in Corsica

La Fuite aux Agriates situates the adventures of a rebellious young woman, Francesca, in the geopolitical and cultural topography of North-Eastern town of Bastia, and the surrounding marsh-like and deserted swamps known as "les Agriates." The novel opens in *media res* with Francesca who just returned from the Agriates where she was hiding with her lover Julius because he murdered a prefect.[8] The narrative sequence of the novel seemingly reconstitutes blurred facts from Francesca's perspective without ever completely aligning to form a clear and coherent story line. The entire town is deeply moved by the tragic end the events took when Julius is found shot dead by an unknown individual. Francesca is being singled out and

---

l'artiste, l'esclave de la loi de réalité, improvise un art dont la nouveauté esthétique a pour fonction de donner forme possible à l'espoir, en manifestant à sa communauté par l'exemple de son engagement esthétique, à l'instar de l'esclave enfui en marronnage, la possibilité d'émergence, entre doute et croyance, des genèses nocturnes renaissantes au son du tambour-Ka »] (Maximin, 41-42 ; my emphasis added in bold).

[8] It can safely be assumed that the blurred references to political terrorism refer to the assassination of prefect Claude Erignac February 6, 1998, which is situated in a period Andreani's study describes as a moment of pivotal violence.

severely critiqued by several women for her affair with Julius, who was actually her sister's fiancé.

Beaten and punished by her mother for her shameful and un-ethical behavior, Francesca attempts suicide and is hospitalized. The family's chambermaid Clorinde takes pity on the young woman and decides to take care of Francesca, who is in an alarming physical state, to the point that she has to be strapped to the bed in order for her body to heal. Francesca slowly recovers but is tortured by nightmares until one night, she finally verbalizes her nightmares of the scene of the crime Julius confessed to being responsible for. The novel closes unexpectedly, with a short exchange between Francesca and her childhood friend, Joseph, in which he admits to having killed Julius for Francesca's sake. Joseph's unexpected confession is as surprising as the fact that Francesca is the only person, who has known all along that the unidentified individual, who killed her lover Julius, is actually Joseph, because he knows about their affair and is deeply in love with Francesca.

In this rather untypical example of Ferranti's fictional writing, violence becomes a narrative event to relate how the human body bears the marks of anti-institutional acts of terror and crime. Contra-ry to Mérimée's "Colomba," Ferranti presents crime and terror as an ontological priority in a masculine world where male heroes, hunters, and killers are glorified. Corsican heroes have a different sense of adventure than the African Friday of the French Caribbean. This type of attitude naturally permeates all realms of island life and par-ticularly affects women whereas in Mérimée's short story, Colomba was presented as the fearless leading figure of a group of ruthless male outlaws, yet, she was deprived of her sexuality, which is clearly not the case for Ferranti's Francesca.

The reader is confronted with the radical decisions of characters without there being any specific signs or explanation to account for the origin of and motive for any of their actions. Between the com-plicated relationships that govern Francesca's and Julius's interac-tions on the one hand, and the political upheaval around terrorist attacks on the other hand, the atmosphere on the island is charged with dramatic tension such as heat, panic, and distress. None of the characters is willing to change or to enter into what Glissant called *la Relation*. While the violent behavior patterns of the male characters match the gallery of characters typically displayed in colonial dis-courses about the Corsican tradition of the vendetta, Ferranti com-bines her characters' disposition for violence with a violent postcolonial discourse about the island that leaves very little room for poetic sentimentality.[9] The landscape of the Agriates is hostile and dangerous for those who do not know their way around, which seemingly replicates the dramatic nature of events in Bastia. All crime and violence is motivated by the rejection of change while resistance is organized through a system of silence that secretly operates on the island, rather than a system of silence that is imposed from the top down as an instrument of oppression. Both Julius and Pierre operate on this principle of silence when it comes to both women and politics, which are seemingly aligned. However, a similar system governs the world of women and their interactions. Silence itself becomes an act of violent resistance and reaches a dangerous culminating point during Julius's funeral, with his mother's monotonous scream-like chant that almost dehumanizes her. This is a dangerous sign which foreshadows the ferocious tradition of internal violence known as *la vendetta* which tends to be initiated by female voices—from the underground.

In conclusion, Ferranti's text shows that violence is more than just a reaction to colonial oppression, conquest, and assimilation. The author draws a connection between honor and violence that does not quite match the anti-colonialist discourse on violence as a means to fight colonialism that psychiatrist, philosopher, and author Frantz Fanon hailed in his 1961 essay, *Les Damnés de la terre [The Wretched of the Earth]*. Ferranti seemingly bypasses the question of legitimacy and constructive re-activation of fragments that tends to drive other postcolonial narratives by illustrating how the act of making explicit physical violence an ontological priority to eliminate difference can cause damage and harm. She does, however, give voice to the female community that unanimously comments on the disempowering effects of terrorism on the island community, thus capturing the essence of rewriting violent histories of the island that the Creolistes movement exclusively relegated to the realms of male writers.

---

[9] "Ah! Mon Dieu! Quand tout cela finira-t-il? Tous ces meurtres, cette folie! Que de morts! » (143) laments Santa Marietti, one of Clorinde's friends.

Works Cited

Andreani, Jean-Louis. *Comprendre la Corse.* Paris: Gallimard, 2010.

Benítez, Rojo A. *The Repeating Island: The Caribbean and the Postmodern Perspective.* Durham: Duke University Press, 1992.

Bernabé, Jean, Chamoiseau, Patrick, and Confiant, Rafaël. *Éloge de la Créolité: Edition bilingue français/anglais.* Transl. M B. Taleb-Khyar. Paris: Gallimard, 1993.

Bongie, Chris. *Islands and Exiles: The Creole Identities of Post/Colonial Literature.* Stanford: Stanford University Press, 1998.

Ces Îles où l'on parle français. Paris: Hérodote, 1985.

Ferranti, Marie. *La Fuite aux Agriates.* Paris: Gallimard, 2000.

---. *Une haine de Corse.* Paris: Gallimard, 2012.

Frantz, Fanon. *Les Damnés de la terre.* Paris: La Découverte, 2002.

Glissant, Édouard. *Discours antillais.* Paris: Gallimard, 2007.

---. *Intention poétique.* Paris: Seuil, 1969,

Maximin, Daniel. *Les Fruits du cyclone: une géopoétique de la Caraïbe.* Paris: Seuil, 2006.

McCusker, Maeve and Soares, Anthony. "Islanded Identities: Constructions of Postcolonial Cultural Insularity." *Islanded Identities: Constructions of Postcolonial Cultural Insularity.* Eds. Maeve McCusker and Anthony Soares. Amsterdam and New York, Rodopi, 2011, pp. xi-xxviii.

Meistersheim, Anne. «Insularité, insularisme, îléité, quelques concepts opératoires.» *Les îles malgré l'Europe.* Ed. IDIM. Bastia: Materia Scritta, 2006, p. 159-179.

---. *Territoire et insularité: le cas de la Corse.* Paris: Publisud, 1991.

Renucci, Janine. *La Corse.* Paris: Presses Universitaires de France, 2001.

THE TASTE OF VIOLENCE: SENSES, SIGNS, BIBLICAL AND THEOLOGICAL ALLUSION IN THE SERVICE OF DRAMATIZATION OF HISTORY: PIERRE MATTHIEU'S *GUISIADE*

Christine McCall Probes and Martine Le Glaunec Landis

In a recent study, anthropologist David Le Breton affirms that "taste is a product of history" and reminds us that historians Lucien Febvre and Robert Mandrou have drawn up a cartography of sensorial culture for the Renaissance.[1] Historians of mentalities and sociologists recognize the contribution of societies, even cities to the notion of taste.[2]

For Philippe Erlanger, the taste of the city of Paris contributed heavily to the crimes of autumn 1572. He insists on the festive atmosphere of that city due to the celebrations and wedding ceremony of Marguerite de Valois and Henri de Navarre—an atmosphere that Erlanger judges to be a factor in the Massacre of Saint Bartholomew's Day, describing it dramatically: "Paris a la fièvre: Paris s'agite: Paris gronde comme un orage" (143). Recent investigations, those of Denis Crouzet and Arlette Jouanna, for example, continue to emphasize the role of taste, the collective spirit, and a mental process, the latter a term used by Jacques Sémelin in his reflections on massacre.[3] For Sémelin, among other critics, the senses participate in the

---

[1] *La Saveur du monde: une anthropologie des sens* (Paris: Métailié, 2006) 40, 330. Subsequent references will appear in the text of this article.

[2] The recent monograph by Jukka Gronow, *The Sociology of Taste* (Routledge, 1997), is a plea for an "aesthetic sociology" which would devote more attention to "communities of taste."

[3] See Denis Crouzet, *Les Guerriers de Dieu: La violence au temps des troubles de Religion, vers 1525-vers 1610* (Champ Vallon, 1990) 2 vols.; Arlette Jouanna, *La Saint-Barthélemy: Les mystères d'un crime d'état* (Gallimard, 2007); Jacques Sémelin, "L'Utilisation politique des massacres", *Revue internationale de politique comparée* 8.1 (2001): 7-22 and "Analyser le massacre: Réflexions comparatives" *Questions de recherches/ Research in question* 7 (September 2002): 1-42 <http://www.ceri-sciences-po.org/publica/qdr.htm> (see, in particulier, his discussion of "processus mental" at pages 12 and 13).

construction of the enemy's identity by a rhetoric of impurity and pollution or of the imaginary which "sees" an Other to destroy ("Analyser . . ." 11-12). According to Le Breton, the conjunction of the senses is so essential to perception that he has proposed the following alternative to the Cartesian formula: "je *sens*, donc je suis" (13). The sensorial is accordingly intimately linked to signification. In this spirit then, our study examines, in a prominent dramatization of massacre, the taste of violence conveyed through the sensorial and the theological, the latter element constituting, to use Le Breton's terminology, a symbolic system fundamental to the Renaissance, shared with members of a community (15).

How is the violence of the French Renaissance, specifically in and around the Saint Bartholomew's Day Massacre, remembered in an important dramatization of the time, the *Guisiade*, written in 1589 by Pierre Matthieu, a young lawyer of only twenty-five years of age who would in 1594 become Henri IV's historiographer? By what rhetorical strategies is the taste of violence, manifest in the historical acts and record, interpreted and memorialized for the stage? Let us recall only a few pertinent examples of this period of mass violence: royal edicts such as the one of 1535 calling for the extirpation and extermination of the Lutheran sect; spectacles of conspirators, hung, their bodies exposed to public view; and finally the great massacre of Huguenots in the night of 23 to 24 August 1572, and on into the "season" of Saint-Bartholomew with further massacres through October in numerous cities such as Angers, Bourges, Lyon, Rouen, Bordeaux and Toulouse.[4]

Signs, symbols and theological allusion fuse, in a rhetoric of violence, to reenact, in Matthieu's dramatic creation, the physical and mental violence of momentous historical events. Pierre Matthieu's aim is two fold: to paint Henri de Guise as the champion of the True Faith and to demonize Henri III. The difference between a legitimate king and a tyrant is a debate "that became the common property of the most outspoken subjects of the King of France" from 1560 to 1600 (Mandrou 122). The League added the doctrine of tyrannicide to the debate. For the monk Jacques Clément and his supporters, the assassination of Henri III, six months after the murder of the Balafré was a righteous deed. Mandrou characterizes the French of the time

---

[4] Janine Garrison in her seminal study *Les Protestants au XVIe siècle* (Paris: Fayard, 1988) has sketched out a "calendar" of Saint-Bartholomew massacres on the map of France, 283.

as a people with a taste for strong emotions and a hypersensitivity of temperament. Our systematic examination of the signs, symbols, and theological allusion in Matthieu's remarkable Renaissance dramatization of contemporary history will demonstrate their crucial role as keys to unlock both meaning and structure. Our focus on Matthieu's characterization of the eponymous personage as a hero of epic dimension will serve to illuminate the playwright's dramatization of atrocities.

Pierre Matthieu's *La Guisiade*, a dramatization of the assassination of the Duc de Guise, has been enjoying something of a revival, thanks to Louis Lobbes's 1990 edition and the scholarship of critics such as Heather Ingman (1985), Gilles Ernst (1985), Olivier Millet (1997), and Jean-Claude Ternaux (2008). *La Guisiade* is currently being acclaimed as an exceptional tragedy, perhaps the only perfect one of all the French Renaissance (Lobbes 52, 54). This *tragédie-crise*, remarkable for its unity of action, has a double objective according to Lobbes, "stigmatiser la personne du monarque et . . . justifier la révolte des ultra catholiques" (Lobbes 20-25, 12). The elements examined in our study are crucial to this double objective. We will, in the interest of time, focus on the Guise.

Since Antiquity the senses have been considered essential to art, literature, and the understanding. Aristotle associates the senses, the sensations, the perception and the arts, declaring that the imagination cannot exist without sensations (2.5, 3.3). St. Augustine, marveling about the prodigious power of memory, emphasizes the importance of the senses as transmitters of images to memory and, basing his reasoning on the classic biblical text of Romans 1:20, links sensory perception to theological understanding and moral judgment.

The allusions in the following verses of the *Guisiade* provide insight into the character of the duke seen as a Davidic warrior willing to die for the faith, and equating faith with the Catholic cause, allegorizing it as the doorkeeper of Heaven: LA ROINE MERE. "Saül en tua mille, un seul David dix milles" (2.1).

LE DUC DE GUISE. Ah! Je mourroy content, estant seur qu'avec moy
Periroit l'Heresie, et renaistroit la Foy:
Foy portiere du ciel, la seule thresoriere
Des graces et des biens de l'immense lumiere.

Je veux mourir pour elle . . . (4.2)[5]

The Duke's words connecting grace and faith would have reminded a biblically informed audience of passages such as Ephesians 2: 8, although it is the Reformed faith that the duke seeks to extirpate that holds dear that passage: "For it is by grace that you have been saved, through faith, and this not from yourselves, it is the gift of God, not by works, so that no one can boast."

If *La Guisiade* presents Henri III with an ambiguity which is supported by biblical and theological allusions (Henri represents himself as a mighty cedar tree, a metaphor for the righteous "planted in the house of the Lord," Psalm 92:12, but he is pronounced a "second Caïn" by the Guise's mother as she learns of her son's assassination), the play presents its eponymous hero in a manner essentially univocal. Matthieu evokes the king's suspicions about the duke's ambition and treachery by the intense mobilization of the sense of touch, highly appropriate to the scene's violence: "les Guisards . . . remuent les couteux meurtierement tranchans" (177-178). These suspicions do not however prevent him from referring to Guise as "ce brave Ligueur" (179). Henri III's testimony is, of course, impugned when he calls on Hell to help him "conjurer la mort" (248) if Heaven will not: "Si le ciel ne le veut, j'ay l'Enfer contre Guise" (400). Espernon, "un homme de si petite valeur, . . . un desesperé, un sorcier, avec toute sa daemonomanie" (acte 3, *argument*, 112), incites his monstrous companions to action: "Jettez sur Blois l'horreur de vos traits effroyables / . . . Changez Blois en Enfer" (802, 805). This character which Matthieu put in the play reluctantly, offers his soul to the demons in exchange for Guise's life, "Je vous offre mon ame . . . / Si . . . / Vous ravissez la vie au chef de ces Ligueurs" (809, 812). But Espernon, even when calling on Satan, "Suffoque, tue, perds tout le sang de Lorraine" (880), cannot help his admiration of the *Guisards*, comparing them to the heroic Jewish patriots of the second century BC, "Preux comme Machabés, forts comme des Cesars" (882). The devil himself, who enters in the fourth act, characterizing the *Guisards* as worse than a pagan army and ascribing to them a "perfide arrogance" (1529), recognizes the esteem in which Guise is

[5] Louis Lobbes, *Pierre Matthieu. La Guisiade* (Geneva: Droz, 1990). Subsequent references will indicate acts, scenes or verses in the text of the article, or, in the case of the *argument*, pages.

held, "Il a gaigné le cueur du peuple et de l'Eglise: / On leve le cha-
peau quand on parle de Guise" (1669-70).

The spectator/reader becomes acquainted with the duke at the
very first scene of *La Guisiade*. The playwright has spoken, in the
argument, of his clear conscience, "ardent zele," "entreprise franche,"
and of "les travaux de ses ancestres . . . pour le bien de la France."
The duke begins his monologue with a description of the Christian
heart, contrasting it with the temptations of the world and "un sen-
tier oblique" (6). The inverse allusion is inescapable. God's way is the
straight path, as numerous biblical passages attest. The Psalmist prays,
for example: "Teach me your way, O Lord; lead me in a straight path"
(Psalm 27: 11). The duke contrasts those who succumb to temptation, opening the door to vice and covering their sins with the holy
cloak of faith, to his own followers "qui ont au cueur ce qu'ils mon-
strent au front, / Me suyvent où le droict, et l'hasard nous semont"
(15-16). For Guise, the path is often a victorious one. As he depicts
his assaults on the Protestants, he repeatedly affirms his triple motivation, "Pour la foy, pour mon Roy, pour defendre ma terre" (33).
Humility seems to characterize him; to God alone is the glory (65-66).
The honor, as well:

> Mais l'honneur est à vous, ô Monarque eternel,
> Je ne suis que soldat, vous estes Coronnel.
> Sous les rais flamboyans de vostre saincte face,
> On me voit rayonner plein d'amour et de grace. (35-38)

The application of the sensorial is varied and multiple from the
inception of the play; the appeal to the sense of sight undergirds descriptions of God as well as that of the duke whose reputation is expressed in sensorial terms: "on m'a veu tousjours au son de la
trompette./ . . ./ On m'a veu balaffré ensanglanter le champ" (41-44).
Metaphorical taste is used at times in a positive manner and at other
times negatively to convey the duke's motivation; if he insists that he
does not "gourmande . . . le lis François", he proclaims as well that
"ses délices sont aux combats et aux armes" (28, 46). Similar sensorial formulae depict his avowed enemies: the king himself: "Le Roy
couve en son cueur un desir inhumain,/ De paistre ses mignons de
tout le sang Lorrain" and the protestants who "d'un vain appetit"
wish to "desmembrer" the monarchy (103-104, 61). The dramatist
employs distaste as well as taste to represent metaphorically the

protestants, the king declaring: "Ce tige monstrueux regerme par mes villes/ Autant qu'on voit l'esté de puantes chenilles" (627-628).

The choir, closing act one, echoes the duke's reliance on God in a highly symbolic allusion to his mighty arm, a commonplace in Old Testament accounts of Israelite victories, Deuteronomy 7: 19, for example:

> Le ciel n'a donné pourtant
> Aux ennemis le triomphe:
> Son bras pour nous combattant,
> Fait que l'Eglise triomphe. (157-60)

The duke twice alludes to God's victory over the giants. Editor Lobbes glosses these verses as a "fleur de rhétorique" typical of the Renaissance and referring to the theogony of ancient mythology (173, 213). We believe he is correct about the second case where Guise remembers "la fin des Geans / Qui leverent le front contre les Dieux puissans" (1869-70). Note first that "Dieux" is plural. In the following line Guise prays to his God, the singular "mon Dieu," that he would not have the prideful and offensive thought of revolt against his king. Our examination of the first case, however, leads us to believe that it is a reference to giants in Old Testament passages such as Deuteronomy 2 and 3, Joshua 12:4 and I Chronicles 20. Guise is asking God to equip his soldiers' arms with force and their hearts with courage (81). Here, God is the singular and more familiar "Pere," and it is his Word "dont l'effort a jadis combattu / Des Geans forcenez l'arrogante vertu" (79-80). The visual and the auditory combine to evoke, in a manner both succinct and efficient, the power of the divine Word: "Pere, qui d'un seul mot faictes trembler le pole/ Comme un foudre sur eux jettez vostre parole" (77-78).

Repeatedly Guise describes his cause in terms of devotion: to the faith, to the church, to God, to France, to the King. The Queen Mother similarly characterizes the cause to her son; the description culminates in a striking apostrophe which is at the same time the first of eight lines, in reality *hémistiches*, of *stichomythie* where she debates with her son the motivation of the cause:

> Ce n'est qu'un pur devoir, qu'une agreable envie,
> Qu'ils ont de conserver vostre lis, vostre vie.
> O amour singulier!
> LE ROY. O belle ambition!
> LA ROINE MERE. Ce n'est qu'un zele entier.

LE ROY. Ce n'est que fiction.
LA ROINE MERE. Dieu juge le dedans.
LE ROY. Je lis dedans leurs ames.
LA ROINE MERE. Ils sont grands et puissans.
LE ROY. De sac, de feu, de flammes. (289-94)

The Cross, symbol and sign of the central doctrine of Christianity--Christ's atonement, represents the standard or banner of the Guise's cause. For the Queen Mother it is a banner that France has held high for 1200 years. In holding high the Cross, the *Guisiens* preserve "La foy par sainct Denis amplement espanie" (282). The appeal to St. Denis, the first Bishop of Paris who christianized the Ile de France, falls on the deaf ears of Henri who, as we recall, resolves, lacking the support of Heaven, to take up Hell against Guise (400). In an exchange with the king the Guise attacks his laxness, "Vostre douceur de tous est jà trop outragee" (616), and insists on harsh measures, "Apres un doux remede il y faut un cautere" (612). Sign and symbol join with touch to convey the violence of the Guise's recommendation of a double *étendard*, the Cross and the Sword (or *baston*)[6]:

> Aux extremes tourmens le remede est extreme.
> Pour en vous conservant garder ce diademe,
> Il ne se faut aider de la Croix simplement:
> Mais il faut du baston combattre vaillamment. (631-34)

The Christian symbolism of the duke's armor warrants a study in itself. A just or good conscience is basic to the equipment of the duke and his followers: "Ils font paroistre à tous leur juste conscience" (419), affirms the Queen Mother. According to St. Paul in I Timothy 1: 19, "holding on to faith and a good conscience" is essential to fighting "the good fight." St. Paul's martial imagery is a metaphor for the Christian life, while for the playwright the battle is, as well, a physical one of swords and blood. When the duke prepares himself to appear before the king who, as recompense for his valor-

---

[6] "Baston" in the following verses suggests a double violence, since in the Renaissance the word could signify "un épieu" or spear, "une épée" or sword, or, as Randle Cotgrave's tells us, "any weapon of offence", *A Dictionarie of the French and English Tongues* (London: Islip, 1611).

ous exploits "empoisonne l'honneur de nostre renommee" (106), his conscience is his shield:

> J'iray parler au Roy: ma saine conscience
> Me servira tousjours de targue et de deffence. (121-22)

If the shield represents his conscience in the lines quoted above, elsewhere it is a metaphor for faith (101). Numerous passages suggest to the reader St. Paul's classic exposition on the armor of God in Ephesians 6: 10-17.

> Finally, be strong in the Lord and in his mighty power. Put on the full armor of God so that you can take your stand against the devil's schemes. For our struggle is not against flesh and blood, but against the rulers, against the authorities, against the powers of this dark world and against the spiritual forces of evil in the heavenly realms. Therefore put on the full armor of God, so that when the day of evil comes, you may be able to stand your ground, and after you have done everything, to stand. Stand firm then, with the belt of truth buckled around your waist, with the breastplate of righteousness in place, and with your feet fitted with the readiness that comes from the gospel of peace. In addition to all this, take up the shield of faith, with which you can extinguish all the flaming arrows of the evil one. Take the helmet of salvation and the sword of the Spirit, which is the word of God.

Matthieu adapts the passage liberally; he keeps the shield of faith, but the Guise's breastplate is characterized not by "righteousness" but by the closely related quality, "holy virtue": "Celuy qui est armé de la forte cuirasse, / De la saincte vertu ne craint ny la menace, / Ny le courroux leger d'un Prince" (1863-65). Virtue is also the duke's standard. As the choir laments his decision to appear before the king as commanded, it sings the duke's praises and foretells the crime which will take place between acts 4 and 5:

> Ah! Prince l'espoir de la France
> Où vas tu? retorne helas!
> . . . .
> Mais l'ame droicte, et sans fainte,
> Sous l'estendart de vertu

Presente le sein sans crainte
De la mort au dard pointu. (1879-80, 1891-94)

If the sense of touch expresses metaphorically the weapon of death, the visual interprets the renown and power of the duke and the Cardinal de Guise, "deux flambeaux, dont la lumiere/ Claire luisoit aux François" (1907-1908). It is perhaps on the basis of biblical texts such as Hebrews 11: 1, I Corinthians 13: 13, Psalm 146: 5 and Colossians 1: 27, that Matthieu adds "hope" to the duke's arsenal. The duke and his father have accomplished their valorous exploits, "targué de foy, et cresté d'esperance" (101). As the messenger recounts the assassination in detail to the duke's mother, he describes a hero who goes to his death armed with virtue and faith, emboldened by his duty and love for the king (2051-2052).

The duke, armed with faith, virtue, and hope, is certainly a hero of epic dimensions. The play's title suggests as much. When the king orders him killed, the choir apostrophizes the sun, calling on Nature to produce an eclipse symbolic of the eclipse of faith, peace and justice that will occur at the duke's death. The visual appeal is double, as the rhetorical strategy of antithesis (lampe, beau jour/ obscur, éclipse) brings out the opposition between the duke, "respecté . . . comme pere de la patrie [et] aymé de tous pour la cause qu'il deffend", and the king of whom the *argument* of the scene remarks "la perfide et inouye vengeance [et] vaine jalousie" (156-157). The opposition is also present in the spirit of the king who admits "deux contraires efforts assaillent mes esprits" before abandoning himself to the taste of violence and resolving: "Il le faut donc tuer: je ne puis avoir pire" (1992).

Pourquoy, ô lampe du beau jour!
Ne rends-tu ton obscur eclipse?
Aujourd'hui eclipse en la Cour
La Foy, la Paix, la Justice. (1999-2002)

The Renaissance spectator/reader would quickly draw the parallel between Jesus' vindication by an eclipse as recorded in the Gospel accounts of his crucifixion and that proposed by the choir at the death of the Guise. Finally, the *argument* of act 5 designates the duke as "ce genereux martyr" (161).

Given the subject of the *Guisiade*, it is hardly surprising to find that biblical and theological allusions permeate the text and contribute to the dramatic representation of the violent events of French history from July to December 1588. A varied and repeated sensorial appeal conveys the taste of violence in dramatic terms and implicates the French public in this violence by means of the play's reading and performance. For example, the diabolical Espernon calls upon Satan's rage to pour itself out on the Guise's partisans: "Bruyez, courez, craquez et portez en vos mains/ Le fer, le feu, l'effroy, pour troubler les humains:/ Guidez, executez mon horrible entreprise,/ . . . / Jettez sur Blois l'horreur de vos traits effroyables:/. . . / Changez Blois en Enfer" (787-789, 802, 805).

Our systematic examination has demonstrated that senses and signs join to biblical and theological allusions to contribute to the development of opposing characters of the plays and can even accentuate their ambiguity, which is the case of Henri III. We have noted that conflicting biblical images, such as the cedar and Cain, underscore the king's character. When the choir uses biblical and theological allusions, they may anticipate action, such as the striking case of the eclipse, announcing the *dénouement* itself.

These strategies heighten dramatic tension as they occur in figures such as apostrophes and metaphors, rime-words, or in theatrical techniques such as *stichomythie*. Let us listen to the intense exchange between Henri III and his mother, Catherine de Médicis, on the character of Guise. The king has announced his "sanglante vengeance sur la sainte ligue des Princes" (acte 2, *argument*, 81):

LE ROY. O belle ambition!
LA ROINE MERE. Ce n'est qu'un zele entier
LE ROY. Ce n'est que fiction.
LA ROINE MERE. Dieu juge le dedans.
LE ROY. Je lis dedans leurs ames.
LA ROINE MERE. Ils sont grands et puissans.
LE ROY. De sac, de feu, de flammes. (292-294)

The constant appeal to the senses, both literal and metaphorical, privileging the visual and the auditory, underscores the bloody atmosphere, the conspiracies and the brutal actions. Thirst signifies ambition and sight triggers memory. The sensorial and the theological intermingle in a rhetoric of violence which may contribute to irony. We hope to have modestly contributed to the analysis of a work which is presently enjoying renewed critical attention[7] as we have illuminated key dramatic strategies which undergird and enrich the taste of violence in this "pièce d'actualité", a dramatic canvas which invites today's reader to reflect on conscience, honor, valor, duty, ambition and faith.

Works Cited

Aristotle. *De Anima.* Paris: Ernest Leroux, 1900.

Augustine. *Confessions.* 2 vols. Paris: Les Belles Lettres, 1998.

---. *De Doctrina Christiana.* Paris: Institut d'Études Augustiniennes, 1997.

Cotgrave, Randle. *A Dictionarie of the French and English Tongues.* London: Islip, 1611.

Crouzet, Denis. *Les Guerriers de Dieu: La violence au temps des troubles de Religion, vers 1525-vers 1610.* 2 vols. Seyssels: Champ Vallon, 1990.

Erlanger, Philippe. *Le Massacre de la Saint-Barthélemy.* Paris: Gallimard, 1960.

Ernst, Gilles. "Des deux *Guisiade* de Pierre Matthieu." *Bibliothèque d'Humanisme et Renaissance* 47 (1985): 367-78.

Garrison, Janine. *Les Protestants au XVIe siècle.* Paris: Fayard, 1988.

---

[7] See, for example: Olivier Millet, "L'Assassinat politique sur la scène au temps des guerres de religion: trois pièces d'actualité." *Vives Lettres* 4 (1997): 7-44; Louis Lobbes, "Pierre Matthieu, dramaturge phénix (1563-1621)." *Revue d'histoire du théâtre* 50 (1998): 207-236; Gilles Bertheau, "Les figures du Duc de Guise et d'Henri III chez George Chapman, Christopher Marlowe et Pierre Matthieu" in *Formes littéraires du théologico-politique de la Renaissance au XVIIIe siècle, Angleterre et Europe. Actes du Colloque de Clermont-Ferrand, 19-21 septembre 2002*, eds. Jean Pironon et Jacques Wagner (Clermont-Ferrand: CERHAC-Presses Universitaires Blaise Pascal, 2003): 131-148; François de Chantelouve, *Pierre Matthieu:The Tragedy of the Late Gaspard de Coligny and the Guisiade*, trans. Richard Hillman (Ottawa: Dovehouse, 2005); George Hoffmann, "France's First Revolution. Hamlet and the 'Unresolved Man' of 1589" in *Civilization in French and Francophone Literature*, eds. Buford Norman and James Day (Amsterdam: Rodopi, 2006), 1-31. See also for the present interest in the dramatization of history: Alain Cullière, "La Saint-Barthélemy au théâtre" in *L'Écriture du massacre en littérature entre l'histoire et mythe. Des mondes antiques à l'aube du XXIe siècle*, ed. Gérard Nauroy (Bern: Lang, 2004), 121-152; *Écritures de l'Histoire (XIVe- XVIe siècles). Actes du Colloque du Centre Montaigne, Bordeaux, 19-21 septembre 2002*, eds. Danièle Bohler et Catherine Magnien Simonin (Geneva: Droz, 2005).

The Geneva Bible. A Facsimile of the 1560 edition. Madison: U of Wisconsin P, 1969.

Gronow, Jukka. *The Sociology of Taste*. London: Routledge, 1997.

Ingman, Heather. "A Study in Ambivalence: Pierre Matthieu's Reading of Machiavelli." *French Studies* 39 (1985): 130-42.

Jouanna, Arlette. *La Saint-Barthélemy: Les mystères d'un crime d'état*. Paris: Gallimard, 2007.

Le Breton, David. *La Saveur du monde: une anthropologie des sens*. Paris: Métailié, 2006.

Lobbes, Louis, éd. *Pierre Matthieu. La Guisiade*. Genève: Droz, 1990.

Mandrou, Robert. *Introduction to Modern France 1500-1640: An Essay in Historical Psychology*. New York: Holmes & Meier, 1976.

Millet, Olivier. "L'Assassinat politique sur la scène au temps des guerres de religion: trois pièces d'actualité." *Vives Lettres* 4 (1997): 7-44.

Sémelin, Jacques. "Analyser le massacre: Réflexions comparatives". *Questions de recherches/ Research in question* 7 (September 2002): 1-42 <http://www.ceri-sciences-po.org/publica/qdr.htm>

---. "L'Utilisation politique des massacres". *Revue internationale de politique comparée* 8.1 (2001): 7-22.

Soman, Alfred, ed. *The Massacre of St. Bartholomew: Reappraisals and Documents*. The Hague: M. Nijhoff, 1974.

Ternaux, Jean-Claude. "La Diabolisation dans *La Guisiade* (1589) de Pierre Matthieu et *Le Guysien* (1592) de Simon Bélyard." *Études Épistémè* 14 (2008): 1-18.

LE ROMAN FAMILIAL DES JARDIN: POUR UNE PSYCHANALYSE DE L'ECRITURE-MIROIR D'ALEXANDRE JARDIN

Sophie Boyer

Dans son livre *Le Nain Jaune* paru en 1978, l'écrivain et scénariste Pascal Jardin (1934-1980) rend un vibrant hommage à son père Jean Jardin (1904-1976), haut fonctionnaire et homme d'affaires décédé deux ans plus tôt. Vers la toute fin de son récit, Jardin-fils relate une scène où ses trois garçons, Emmanuel, Alexandre et Frédéric, expriment leur curiosité face au projet d'écriture de leur père : « Ils attendent de moi des mensonges qui soient vrais, de quoi rêver le jour au milieu de la rue en allant à l'école. Ils attendent de moi que peu à peu, je les fasse, un à un, devenir un peu lui » (196-197). Lui, étant bien sûr le grand-père, Jean Jardin. Or, si quelque trente ans plus tard, Alexandre Jardin, petit-fils de Jean devenu romancier à succès, se reconnaît une gémellité certaine avec son grand-père, il reconnaît surtout l'urgence de mettre fin à son règne de patriarche et, par le fait même, de se dissocier psychiquement de son aïeul en révélant la faute que ce grand-père, autrefois adulé, aujourd'hui honni, a fait porter à tout le clan.

Dans ce qui suit, j'exposerai comment le plus récent ouvrage d'Alexandre Jardin, *Des gens très bien* (2011), se doit d'être interprété comme une double entreprise : entreprise de réécriture d'abord, de son *Roman des Jardin* (2005), voire de toute son œuvre, et entreprise de confession ensuite, confession du lourd passé familial incarné par la personne de son grand-père Jean Jardin, dit le Nain Jaune, directeur de cabinet de Pierre Laval au sein du gouvernement de Vichy au moment de la rafle du Vélodrome d'hiver (16-17 juillet 1942), qui coûta la vie à quelques 13 000 Juifs français.

Je démontrerai d'abord comment, tant dans sa structure narrative que dans ses procédés stylistiques, *Des gens très bien* se donne à lire comme une réplique, un écho inversé au précédent *Roman des Jardin*. Si ce dernier pèche par une esthétique de l'excès caractéristique de toute une œuvre employée à enchanter le réel, *Des gens très bien* marque une rupture de ton définitive et un parti pris pour la gravité. Tout au long de cette exploration de la forme, je livrerai à la fois une lecture parallèle des principaux thèmes abordés ainsi qu'une lecture psychanalytique du propos tenu, consciemment ou non, par Alexandre Jardin dans ses deux ouvrages : ainsi, tandis que *Le Roman des Jardin* se veut une entreprise de déni et de déplacement faisant figure de souvenir-écran dont la première fonction est de refouler le seul véritable enjeu familial – à savoir, la culpabilité du grand-père –, *Des gens très bien* représente une entreprise de confession qui n'est pas sans s'apparenter à une démarche thérapeutique de libération, libération de l'aphasie collective menant ici ultimement au Meurtre du Père.

Dans son *Roman des Jardin*, paru en 2005, Alexandre Jardin dresse une fois de plus[1] un portrait truculent des membres de sa famille et de leurs intimes, portrait amplement nourri par leurs aventures rocambolesques et leurs mœurs dissolues. À titre d'exemples, mentionnons seulement l'épisode où la grand-mère paternelle, l'épouse de Jean Jardin, exige du médecin de famille qu'il lui transfère le ver solitaire, baptisé Zoé, qui rongeait tranquillement les entrailles de la gouvernante Zouzou (« Le ver solitaire de Zouzou » : partie I, chapitre 9); ou encore, le rapport détaillé des amours grotesques et tumultueuses entre Yves Salgues, journaliste et héroïnomane notoire, ami intime des Jardin, et sa guenon Zaza (« La guenon de Salgues » : partie I, chapitre 10). Or, Jardin insiste d'entrée de jeu sur le caractère *romanesque* de ce récit autobiographique : il affiche en effet un net penchant pour la fiction, posture d'autant plus justifiée que le clan Jardin semble toujours s'être fait un honneur de mettre en scène son quotidien, d'en faire, aux dires de l'auteur, un « vaudeville familial » (17). À force de passer en revue les faits et gestes insolites du bestiaire Jardin, un portrait d'ensemble se dégage : la famille Jardin se révèle ainsi un véritable « musée d'anomalies » (20) peuplé d'individus ayant érigé en valeurs suprêmes la liberté, l'excès et l'originalité; tous, ils tiennent à se distinguer de ceux qu'ils appellent avec mépris « les normaux » dont le destin est nécessairement marqué par le travail, l'accumulation du capital et la monogamie; en somme, la banalité. En effet, les Jardin semblent adhérer par choix à un mode de vie inspiré de la décadence aristocratique, univers de surfaces s'inscrivant en faux contre la médiocrité de la petite bour-

---

[1] Le système d'échos qui relie *Le Roman des Jardin* à *Des gens très bien* s'étend en fait à bien d'autres des ouvrages d'Alexandre Jardin. Déjà *Le Zubial* (1997), dans son encensement de la figure paternelle et de tout le clan Jardin, annonçait par le choix des anecdotes et une propension à l'hyperbole *Le Roman des Jardin* à venir, au point où le lecteur croirait assister parfois à de l'auto-plagiat.

geoisie. Or, au milieu de ce foutoir de doux dingues, Alexandre admet faire figure d'imposteur, étant intrinsèquement de nature conformiste, en d'autres termes : un « raté de l'absolu » (15), un traître.

Par conséquent, le souvenir d'une enfance déroutante parce que vécue sans aucune forme de balises ou de repères moraux provoque chez l'auteur des sentiments mitigés, oscillant entre admiration et colère. Son *Roman des Jardin* serait, tel que veut nous le faire croire l'auteur, le résultat de cette oscillation, témoignant tant de l'un que de l'autre. Cependant une lecture même superficielle du *Roman des Jardin* mais, surtout, une lecture menée en parallèle avec celle de son prochain ouvrage, *Des gens très bien*, révèle au lecteur que cette volonté d'équilibre n'est qu'un leurre : *Le Roman des Jardin* se situe uniquement dans l'admiration et la célébration de la folie des siens tandis que *Des gens très bien* creuse le seul sillon de la colère et du ressentiment, émotions suscitées par une lucidité tardive. Ainsi, par un bizarre jeu de miroirs et d'échos, l'un se révèle l'envers de l'autre, son double inversé en quelque sorte, à l'instar de la figure médiatique que représente Alexandre Jardin d'ailleurs : en effet, de l'Alexandre qui rit, puéril homme-enfant qui se cache derrière un « rire bouclier » (*Roman* 146), nous passons en 2011, dans le cadre de la promotion de *Des gens très bien*, à Alexandre qui pleure, un homme au visage grave, à la moue crispée, sérieuse, apparaissant vieilli tout à coup, incarnant l'abandon de toute mascarade.

Au cœur des deux ouvrages se manifeste le même souci de donner un sens au projet d'écriture. Ainsi, dès le préambule au *Roman des Jardin*, l'écrivain se fait admirateur, présentant son livre comme « un manifeste en faveur des Jardin » (31); le ton du rire, de la légèreté, de l'enchantement, bref, du mensonge, est donné : « C'est cela pour moi, écrire : riposter, se supposer l'âme d'un irréductible, pratiquer en mousquetaire le refus de l'indigeste réalité » (31). En ce sens, nous avons affaire avec *Le Roman des Jardin* à un véritable « roman familial » au sens freudien du terme, fantasmagorie de l'enfant s'imaginant des parents autres, idéalisés (Laplanche 427), car de fait, la famille sera ici encensée, ses mœurs exposées mais jamais remises en question et ses tares toujours habilement dissimulées. Quant à *Des gens très bien*, plus question d'y « jardiniser » le réel; ici, l'écriture devient entreprise de vérité, devoir de lucidité et ultimement, acte de renaissance. Ainsi, le même auteur, intimement convaincu de livrer avec son *Roman des Jardin* un « livre intègre », de s'adonner par ses aveux à un « exercice d'honnêteté » (*Roman* 16), reniera cinq ans plus tard sa pratique d'un soi-disant « mentir vrai » (*Gens* 114), posture de refus volontaire de la réalité révélée soudain comme véritable *im-posture* justement. *Le Roman des Jardin* est divisé en trois parties intitulées : I. La comédie, II. L'addition et III. Survivre. *Des gens très bien* est également divisé en trois parties : I. Fini de rire, II. Se refaire et III. Entretien avec le pire. Or, chacune des parties du *Roman des Jardin* trouve un prolongement thématique, une sorte de réponse, d'écho inversé dans la partie correspondante de *Des gens très bien*. Je dis écho inversé, car d'un ouvrage à l'autre, plutôt que de perdre en acuité, le propos au contraire se précise et le ton s'affine pour mieux atteindre la cible, un peu comme si après avoir lancé un caillou dans l'eau, le mouvement des cercles concentriques s'inversait. À cet égard, le leitmotiv du dé-doublement et de l'inversion sous toutes ses formes agit comme une subtile mise en abyme de cet effet miroir qu'exercent l'un sur l'autre les deux ouvrages : en effet, Jardin insiste à maintes reprises sur le fait que plusieurs membres de sa famille sont ambidextres ou souf-frent d'une malformation les dotant de deux rates – d'où leur carac-tère particulièrement hilare – mais, plus près encore de la pratique d'écriture que j'essaie de cerner ici, il insiste sur le don que possède son oncle Merlin, gaucher miroir, pour l'écriture spéculaire[2]. Or, j'avancerais ici que *Des gens très bien*, c'est en quelque sorte *Le Roman des Jardin* écrit de la main sinistre d'Alexandre Jardin[3].

« La comédie », première partie du *Roman des Jardin*, met avant tout l'accent sur l'univers théâtral des Jardin, entend métamorphoser la réalité en « mensonge perfectionné » (76); dans *Des gens très bien*,

---

[2] Dans son cinquième roman, *L'île des Gauchers*, Alexandre Jardin met en scène un monde utopique parce qu'à l'inverse du monde ordinaire. Ici, la morosité du quotidien est évacuée et la flamme amoureuse entretenue par un jeu de séduction sans cesse renouvelé – thème récurrent dans l'œuvre de Jardin – et ce, grâce au choix conscient des protagonistes de délaisser le droit chemin pour assumer une vie de gauchers. Or, Jardin révèle dans « Jamais le dimanche » (partie II, chapitre 10 du *Roman des Jardin*) que *L'île des Gauchers* lui fut inspiré de la tradition dominicale de sa famille selon la-quelle les rôles entre maîtres et serviteurs étaient volontairement échangés, véritable monde inversé aux accents étrangement bakhtiniens.

[3] Cette pratique quasi-suicidaire de désaveu de ses propres écrits, Jardin avoue s'y être déjà adonné bien que sous le couvert de l'anonymat quand dans « La guenon de Salgues », chapitre mentionné ci-dessus, il révèle avoir publié simultanément en 1991 son troisième roman, *Fanfan*, bluette au suc-cès fulgurant, et « une sorte d'anti-*Fanfan* » (*Roman* 105), roman policier fort éloigné des bons sentiments auxquels il a habitué ses lecteurs.

cette même comédie est démasquée et révélée pour ce qu'elle est, c'est-à-dire un immense mécanisme de déni de la réalité. La réalité historique des Jardin est triste, horrible, tout sauf drôle; si Alexandre Jardin est pour naître à lui-même, son premier devoir est d'arrêter d'esquiver et surtout d'arrêter de rire comme il se l'exhorte à lui-même : « Mais il faut bien un jour que la comédie cesse » (*Gens* 28). L'envers de la comédie mènera donc logiquement à « Fini de rire », première partie de *Des gens très bien* où l'auteur expose d'entrée de jeu sa théorie sur la morale du Mal, sur ces éponymes gens soit disant très bien dont fut son grand-père :

> Si l'on désire brûler une synagogue, il suffit de rameuter une poignée de canailles sans foi ni loi; mais pour pratiquer un antisémitisme d'État, il est impératif de mobiliser des gens très bien, dotés de vertus morales solides. Les détraqués, les sadiques huileux et les pervers professionnels ne sont pas assez nombreux. Ni suffisamment efficaces. [...] La criminalité de masse reste par définition le fait d'hommes éminemment *moraux*. Pour tuer beaucoup et discriminer sans remords, il faut une éthique. (24-25)

La deuxième partie du *Roman des Jardin*, intitulée « L'addition », fait d'abord référence à la dette que doit payer Alexandre pour tous les excès de sa famille, mais aussi, en filigrane, à la nécessité d'expier la faute du grand-père, de « réparer... Vichy » (185). Le courage de véritablement nommer la faute est toutefois sans cesse court-circuité par un subtil jeu de déplacements. Ainsi, l'intensité de la faute passe à l'arrière-plan et l'attention du lecteur se voit dirigée vers des effets de style, vers un ton hilare, vers une célébration de la dissonance jardinesque supposément génératrice d'esprits créateurs; l'admiration, toujours, doit triompher. Dans « Se refaire », deuxième partie de *Des gens très bien*, Jardin passe à l'acte timidement annoncé dans « L'addition » et tente une réparation à sa manière : d'abord, en rendant hommage aux victimes de la rafle du Vel d'Hiv par une visite spontanée du camp de concentration de Beaune-la-Rolande (« Beaune-la-Rolande » : partie II, chapitre 2); puis, en devenant rien de moins que Juif (« Devenir juif » : partie II, chapitre 6), c'est-à-dire en s'intéressant de près au Talmud; finalement, en enjuivant la France (« Enjuiver la France » : partie II, chapitre 7), c'est-à-dire en s'investissant dans *Lire et faire lire*, programme bénévole pour la promotion de la lecture. Pour expier la faute, Jardin doit d'abord la reconnaître et donc, nécessairement trahir les siens (« De la nécessité de trahir » : partie II, chapitre 10), devenir un exilé, un exclus. En refusant l'aphasie et la cécité, il met un terme à la perpétuation du mensonge et se déleste d'un héritage trop lourd. Le malaise d'être un Jardin, malaise répété *ad nauseam* dans la plupart de ses récits à caractère autobiographique, se traduit pour l'auteur par un désir obsessionnel de se purger de son sang, de son ADN[4] : si, par ses aveux, il gagne en dignité et respect de lui-même, il se voit du même coup refuser son adhésion à la communauté des siens.

Dans la troisième et dernière partie du *Roman des Jardin*, « Survivre », encore une fois, Jardin s'approche de plus en plus du véritable enjeu en évoquant son désir de réparer les erreurs de son grandpère par l'action *Lire et faire lire* mais, encore une fois, il louvoie vers un portrait idéalisé de sa famille et clôt son roman sur le fameux « Registre des amours des Jardin », volume dans lequel sa grand-mère aurait répertorié les amours illicites du clan. On sent cependant l'essoufflement de l'auteur, son manque d'enthousiasme et de conviction soudain à s'exciter pour les frivolités d'une tribu d'excentriques. Ce n'est d'ailleurs sûrement pas un hasard si ce qu'il retient de son excursion au château de son enfance (« Retour à la Mandragore » : partie III, chapitre 9), la Mandragore, est que cette demeure, maintenant vendue et en voie de rénovation, n'est plus qu'une façade : « La falaise minérale de la façade se tenait toujours droite, mais elle semblait un mince décor de cinéma tenu verticalement par des équerres géantes. […] Mon enfance avait été entièrement vidée de son contenu » (294). De fait, le centre névralgique de la vie familiale des Jardin, la Mandragore au bord du lac Léman, est

---

[4] Dans *Le Zubial*, livre-hommage à Pascal Jardin, ce désir exprime avant tout la nostalgie du fils, Alexandre, pour son père décédé et le nécessaire travail du deuil : « Parfois, je voudrais m'ouvrir les veines pour me vider de son sang, et refaire le plein d'ordinaire » (66). Dans *Le Roman des Jardin*, ce désir prend toutefois une autre signification, à savoir la fatigue éprouvée à vivre dans une famille qui érige l'excentricité en diktat : « À quarante ans, j'aimerais parfois me purger de mon sang pour me reposer le cœur, et me remplir enfin d'un sérum stagnant » (54). Finalement, la signification de ce même désir se radicalise quand, dans *Des gens très bien*, l'auteur explique son dégoût de porter les gènes d'un grand-père collaborateur. En effet, suite à la visite du camp de concentration où furent amenées les victimes de la rafle du Vel d'Hiv, une purge au sens littéral devient un besoin impératif : « Je n'ai parlé à personne et suis allé donner mon sang dans un camion de la Croix-Rouge; pour m'extirper de mon malaise, rejoindre le sang des hommes » (180).

littéralement devenu un souvenir-écran, « formation de compromis entre des éléments refoulés et la défense » (Laplanche 451), une surface creuse qui offre en trompe-l'œil l'illusion d'une enfance paradisiaque, parce que justement sans contenu, sans substance. Le contenu, il est libéré du refoulement collectif dans « Entretien avec le pire », troisième partie de *Des gens très bien*, où tel un Pirandello s'entretenant avec sa mère défunte, Jardin imagine pareil entretien avec le Nain Jaune, le pire père imaginable. Là, l'auteur expose « le secret des Jardin » (295) et de petit-fils soumis, il passe au rang du père : en effet, nommer la faute signifie assumer sa révolte face au Père tout puissant jusqu'à le mettre à mort symboliquement pour enfin accéder à la maturité.

Cette lecture en parallèle des deux ouvrages met au jour les mêmes personnages, les mêmes épisodes, les mêmes conflits et enjeux, mais observés tantôt de la perspective admiratrice de l'homme-enfant, tantôt de la perspective critique et encolérée de l'homme-adulte. Tandis que d'un côté, on maquille pour mieux contourner, pour mieux ne pas voir, de l'autre, on dévoile jusqu'à l'os. Ainsi, parmi toutes les anecdotes évoquées, il en existe une qui se doit d'être interprétée comme la *Urszene*, la scène originaire, primitive (Laplanche 432) de la famille Jardin, réellement observée dans *Le Roman des Jardin* et simplement imaginée dans *Des gens très bien* : celle du grand-père dans sa chambre d'hôtel s'adonnant non pas à un quelconque rapport sexuel dont son petit-fils, témoin de la scène, aurait été traumatisé, mais s'adonnant plutôt à une collaboration avec le Mal. Si dans « L'ambidextre » (partie I, chapitre 3 du *Roman des Jardin*), le petit Alexandre assiste, témoin muet, à une scène de financement occulte des partis politiques d'après-guerre dans la suite du Nain Jaune à l'hôtel La Pérouse, il se voit dans « Enfin » (partie III, chapitre 9 de *Des gens très bien*) aller à la rencontre de son grand-père dans son bureau de l'hôtel du Parc le soir du 16 juillet 1942 afin de le convaincre qu'il est encore temps de renverser le cours de l'histoire. Tandis que la première scène sert à souligner avec légèreté l'habileté ambidextre du grand-père, la seconde révèle la face cachée de cette même ambidextrie : à savoir la duplicité, le « cerveau […] inversé » (*Gens* 96), retors de son aïeul. D'un ouvrage à l'autre, toujours le même passage des ténèbres de la cécité vers la lumière de la lucidité, du strass et du spectacle vers la rigueur et la gravité.

Tel que démontré jusqu'à maintenant, l'effet-miroir se fait surtout sentir grâce aux recoupements thématiques, mais j'aimerais donner une dernière fois la mesure de ce même effet-miroir jusque dans la structure même des deux récits, en m'attardant brièvement sur une de ses manifestations. Ainsi, la première partie des deux ouvrages, « La comédie » et « Fini de rire », est chacune ponctuée de trois chapitres intitulés « Zouzou m'a dit » (dans le cas du *Roman des Jardin*) ou « Zac m'a dit » (dans le cas de *Des gens très bien*). D'un côté comme de l'autre, ces chapitres mettent en scène un dialogue soit avec la gouvernante de la famille, Zouzou, témoin lucide de la folie des Jardin, soit avec un ami plus rusé et surtout plus juif que les autres, Zac. Dans les deux cas, il s'agit toujours pour l'auteur d'une confrontation avec la voix de sa conscience. Or, si Zouzou tente à maintes reprises d'ouvrir le jeune Alexandre à la vérité, au passé honteux de sa famille, allant même jusqu'à lui reprocher son manque de courage dans son métier d'écrivain, dans le tout dernier chapitre du *Roman des Jardin*, intitulé aussi « Zouzou m'a dit », le mensonge triomphe quand l'auteur affirme « [s]a volonté de ne pas savoir » (316). Dans *Des gens très bien*, le jeune Alexandre est instruit dans les chapitres « Zac m'a dit » du passé collabo de son grand-père et de l'immense mécanisme de déni orchestré par tout le clan Jardin, mais tout particulièrement par Pascal Jardin qui, dans son ouvrage *Le Nain Jaune* mentionné dans mon introduction, réussit à faire oublier les fautes de son père, Jean Jardin, en l'exhibant comme objet de fierté, supercherie qu'Alexandre s'empresse de dévoiler en affirmant que dans le roman de son père, « récit antitraumatique » (*Gens* 29) par excellence, « le style effaçait le sujet » (*Gens* 40). Tout en saisissant que les reproches adressés ici à son père, Pascal, pourraient tout aussi bien s'appliquer à sa propre tentative de détournement des véritables enjeux, il importe de nuancer quelque peu la proposition « le style effaçait le sujet »; le style maquille le sujet, certes, le recouvre, mais jamais il ne parvient, à mon sens, à le gommer complètement. Les excès verbaux, hyperboles et autres néologismes symptomatiques du *Roman des Jardin*, et de toute l'œuvre d'Alexandre Jardin depuis *Bille en tête*, ont tous pour but de créer un écran de fumée pour mettre à distance un secret de Polichinelle, à savoir l'implication directe du grand-père dans des crimes contre l'humanité et la complicité silencieuse de tout le clan Jardin. La stratégie, utilisée de père en fils, pour faire oublier la réalité est simple : montrer, exhiber le Nain Jaune pour mieux le rendre invisible, protéger la faute du Nain Jaune des regards en la laissant, telle une carte à jouer, là au milieu de la table, subtilement à découvert[5]. C'est d'ailleurs l'ami Zac qui initie le jeune

---

[5] Il est intéressant de noter que le surnom de Jean Jardin, le Nain Jaune, lui

Alexandre à ce mécanisme machiavélique en lui conseillant la lecture du *Séminaire sur la lettre volée* de Jacques Lacan. Dans ce texte mainte-nant célèbre, le psychanalyste français illustre le phénomène de l'automatisme de répétition à partir d'une analyse de la nouvelle d'Edgar Allan Poe, *The Purloined Letter*. Au cœur de l'intrigue et de l'enquête imaginée par Poe se trouve une lettre volée, porteuse d'un message inconnu du lecteur mais dont l'éventuel dévoilement im-plique une menace pour toutes les parties concernées dans l'affaire. Or, dans un dénouement ironique, la lettre que tous cherchaient s'avérera avoir été invisible, parce que justement trop bien à la vue, situation démontrant bien, selon Lacan, la circulation du signifiant – la lettre – et son passage de l'inconscient – la lettre en souffrance, traduction plus littérale de *purloined* – à la conscience – la lettre arri-vant toujours à destination.

À l'instar du ministre dans la nouvelle d'Edgar Allan Poe qui subtilise une lettre lourde de sens et, la sachant recherchée, choisit de la laisser bien à la vue, Jean, Pascal et Alexandre sont tous, effet-miroir oblige, à la fois l'artisan et la dupe de leur propre autrucherie. Un tel constat aurait cependant été sans compter sur la maturité tar-dive qu'affiche Alexandre Jardin en posant, et en nommant surtout, un regard qui voit que son père et son grand-père ont laissé « ce qui est à cacher à découvert pour qui voudra s'en emparer » (Lacan 15). Dans un revers de situation tout lacanien, on peut conclure qu'avec *Des gens très bien*, la lettre volée – pur signifiant du Mal commis par l'un et trop longtemps tu par les autres – arrive enfin à destination.

Ouvrages cités

Jardin, Alexandre. *Bille en tête*. Paris : Gallimard, 1986.
---. *Des gens très bien*. Paris : Grasset, 2010.
---. *Fanfan*. Paris : Flammarion, 1990.
---. *L'île des Gauchers*. Paris : Gallimard, 1995.
---. *Le Roman des Jardin*. Paris : Grasset, 2005.
---. *Le Zubial*. Paris : Gallimard, 1997.
Jardin, Pascal. *Le Nain Jaune*. Paris : Julliard, 1978.
Lacan, Jacques. *Écrits*. Paris : Seuil, 1966.
Laplanche, Jean et J.-B. Pontalis. *Vocabulaire de la psychanalyse*. Paris : Presses universitaires de France, 2002.

---

vient du jeu de cartes du même nom à cause « de sa capacité inouïe à fabri-quer de la chance » (*Roman* 21).

II: IDENTITY, SUBJECTIVITY, AND THE NATIONAL

EL TEATRO VANGUARDISTA CENTROAMERICANO INAUGURAL: PERFORMATIVIDAD E IDENTIDAD EN *CUCULCÁN Y CHINFONÍA BURGUESA*

Alessandra Chiriboga Holzheu

Más allá de la obra vanguardista teatral de Roberto Arlt y Vicente Huidobro, el teatro latinoamericano vanguardista de las primeras décadas del siglo XX, lo que Burger llama la vanguardia histórica, son desconocidas. Las razones son múltiples: su complejidad interpretativa, su supuesta caducidad temática y carácter escapista (categorización que subsiste por el influjo del Realismo Social a partir de la década de 1930), así como el difícil acceso a los mismos textos, la carencia de recursos económicos para llevar estas obras a la escena, entre otras. La Vanguardia, contrario a lo que muchos creen ahora, no sólo fue un movimiento poético, sino fue una cosmovisión que modernizó la expresión artística general desde el cine, la escultura, la pintura, diversos manifiestos y obras teatrales, performances, tertulias, cafés, entre otros. Más que una estética, el movimiento vanguardista llegó a significar la acción y agencia social de la expresión artística: "...the idea of social renewal through cultural challenge rather than by means of overtly political activity" (Cardullo 13)[1]. La van-

---

[1] El espíritu combativo del término "vanguardia" proviene del influjo leninista y su teoría sobre el partido bolchevique como ente encargado de la toma revolucionaria de poder. Esta concepción de una élite revolucionaria dirigente identifica al partido comunista como "la vanguardia de la clase obrera, un grupo consciente, expresión de esa clase, encargado de llevarla a la victoria", pero también conforma una teoría estética que identifica la literatura como un espacio social y político: el Realismo Social (Videla 23). Este movimiento, aunque conformó el método literario oficial soviético a partir de 1934, mantuvo una polémica interna por aquellos que cuestionaban el realismo como método eficaz para la propaganda literaria. Videla asegura que "Estas polémicas en torno a la funcionalidad o no funcionalidad revolucionaria y política del vanguardismo literario se proyectan también en Europa Occidental (Bretón, por ejemplo, adhiere al marxismo pero tiene dificultades con la política cultural soviética) e influirán en Hispanoamérica" (24). Por la prescripción soviética del Realismo Social, la vanguardia estética se vio condenada a considerarse por algunos como un "escapismo formalista", tomando como ejemplo la postura estatal frente a la poesía de Maia-

guardia no sólo fue una estética sino fue una cosmovisión, un modo de ver, vivir, estar y representar diferentes realidades desde un código base maleable.

Síntoma y a la vez efecto del cambio modernizador que se vivía debido a la tecnificación industrial y laboral, la estética experimental vanguardista registró el cambio radical que marcó la transición del siglo XIX al XX (urbanización, inmigración, desarrollo del sistema de transporte y comunicación, etcétera) pero también la problematización de la función social del arte y del artista. El arte pasó no sólo a ser medio de expresión del artista, sino también medio por el cual el artista anheló apelar a las nuevas masas urbanas y criticar a la burguesía, razón por la que la expresión vanguardista buscó integrar elementos de la cultura popular y regional en su repertorio estético. El teatro, escrita expresamente para ser representado frente a un público, rearticuló diferentes subjetividades nacionales y propuso diversas comunidades imaginadas[2].

En el caso centroamericano, la estética vanguardista debe estudiarse y contextualizarse dentro de círculos concéntricos de influen-

---

kovski. En *Poetry of the Revolution: Marx, Manifestos, and the Avant-Gardes* Martin Puchner establece una ruptura en el uso del manifiesto iniciada por el Futurismo italiano, cuando Marinetti, desde una postura fascista, logró reencauzar ("co-opt") el impulso revolucionario de este género de origen socialista. A partir de Marinetti se generó una división entre la postura vanguardista identificada con la revolución político-estética fascista y la socialista (que, a pesar de distinguirse como dos posturas ideológicas separadas, usaron recursos estéticos similares). La distinción principal entre el uso que el vanguardismo italiano y soviético le dieron a esta estética experimental fue que, mientras Marinetti asoció la vanguardia con la guerra, los futuristas soviéticos la asociaron con la revolución (Puchner 81). A pesar de que la Anti-academia nicaragüense haya escrito diversos manifiestos, no los analizaré en el presente trabajo, pero me interesa establecer un paralelo entre el uso que Marinetti le da al manifiesto y un uso similar en esta única agrupación vanguardista centroamericana que ideológicamente se adscribió a un modelo nacionalista autoritario que adoptó el modelo de dictadura corporativista católica de Primo de Rivera en España y de Salazar en Portugal; también recibió influencia de otros modelos de autoritarismo político-católico como el de Charles Maurrás y la Action Française, así como los Nacionalistas argentinos.

[2] Utilizo este término en relación al concepto de Benedict Anderson, que sostiene que una nación es una comunidad construida socialmente, imaginada por las personas que se perciben a sí mismas como miembros de este grupo.

cias: un nivel internacional, uno continental, uno ístmico y, finalmente, el nacional (en sus diversas interpretaciones y proyecciones occidentales y no occidentales). La función del artista y arte latinoamericano se rearticuló desde los parámetros de una renovación del pensamiento humanista/renacentista (tomemos como ejemplo el pensamiento de Ortega y Gasett, Spengler, Nietzsche, Bergson, Einstein) que se agudizó por la Primera Guerra Mundial, pero también desde diversas exigencias de movimientos nacionales (el discurso unionista centroamericano y el sandinismo, por ejemplo). En el ámbito latinoamericano la pérdida de las últimas colonias españolas en 1898, la creciente influencia de los Estados Unidos y la Revolución Mexicana (junto con su movimiento ideológico y cultural pos-revolucionario) influyeron en el pensamiento y expresión cultural, afianzando la necesidad de diferenciar racial y culturalmente a Latinoamérica. En Centro y Sudamérica surgieron movimientos estudiantiles con aspiraciones de renovación sociocultural que abiertamente rechazaron y criticaron posturas e instituciones tradicionales (por ejemplo, el movimiento aprista inaugurado por Haya de la Torre, en México).[3] El pensamiento latinoamericano llegó a un nuevo nivel de deseuropeización nunca antes visto.

---

[3] El movimiento estudiantil que inicialmente representó este interés renovador universitario fue el de Córdova, Argentina, en 1918. En 1921 se organizó el Congreso Internacional de Estudiantes de México desde el 20 de septiembre al 8 de octubre de 1921, coincidiendo con la celebración del centenario de la independencia mexicana (Asturias así como delegados nicaragüenses asistieron a esta conferencia). El congreso no sólo comunicó a la dispersa juventud americana, sino también la puso en contacto con intelectuales como Valle Inclán y José Vasconcelos, por ejemplo, que asistieron a los eventos como representantes honorarios. Este grupo pretendió formular una nueva y renovada organización y movimiento social que permitiera la realización de lo que se percibió como un reordenamiento social con fines morales y espirituales. Fue así como se creó un vínculo entre los intelectuales y estudiantes hispanoamericanos, un nuevo poder social que tratará de vincularse con las masas populares para procurar el desenvolvimiento de un plan de renovación social. Entre estas nuevas redes intelectuales falta mencionar influjos transcontinentales como el de la Internacional de los Intelectuales con las diversas organizaciones estudiantiles latinoamericanas. Anatole France y Henri Barbusse lanzaron su "Manifiesto a los intelectuales y estudiantes de América latina."

El derrocamiento de dictaduras positivistas decimonónicas como la de Porfirio Díaz, Estrada Cabrera y Santos Zelaya, entre otros, modificó la función del arte y del artista en el contexto nacional. El apoyo y mecenazgo que Darío y Santos Chocano, por ejemplo, recibieron de distintos regímenes centroamericanos decimonónicos se volvió una ilusión del pasado, la transitoriedad de los gobiernos desestabilizó el financiamiento estatal de las artes. Muchos Modernistas, junto con su estética, fueron rechazados por las nuevas generaciones al ser asociados negativamente con las dictaduras objetadas y suplantadas por gobiernos que profesaban discursos democráticos. El arte, por ende, intentó independizarse de la administración política nacional, aunque aún ejerció legitimidad social para proveer modelos de identidad nacional.

La primera obra de teatro que me interesa señalar es *Chinfonía burguesa* (1939), de Joaquín Pasos y José Coronel Urtecho, dos representantes de la agrupación vanguardista nicaragüense llamada Anti-academia[4]. *Chinfonía* relata el noviazgo y casamiento fallido de un poeta con Fifí, la hija de un de un mercader llamado Don Chombón. La unión de Fifí con el poeta produce un garrobo o iguana sietemesina generada por un embarazo inesperado. Cuando el padre de Fifí contempla a su nieto, heredero de su fortuna y legado, exclama: "¡Llévate a Jacobo / que es producto del robo / que es una mixtura impura / de la poesía y de la burguesía!". Esta alianza perjudicial se proyecta en la gordura e improductividad del poeta al integrarse a la vida burguesa: "Va engordando el pueta como / una ruleta / Su panza alcanza en una / romanza, / 208 libras puja la balanza. / Ya está curado de los pies- / quebrados, / le ha nacido un bigote / en lugar del estrambote / y se han pulverizado los / esqueletos de sus sonetos". La unión entre Fifí y el Pueta adquiere una cualidad de ficción fundacional infecunda por sus mismas causas de la unión. Fifí objetiviza al poeta y este, a cambio, se interesa por el dinero de Don Chombón: "Fifí (coqueta) / ¡Non! / (pizpereta) / La caja de caudales

---

[4] La fecha inaugural oficial del movimiento de Vanguardia Nicaragüense es el 17 de abril de 1931, fecha en la que el periódico *El Diario Nicaragüense*, órgano oficial del partido Conservador, publicó el manifiesto *Ligera exposición y proclama de la anti-academia nicaragüense*. A pesar de ser una obra colectiva que reúne los nombres de diez autores nicaragüenses, sobresale en la historiografía literaria nacional los nombres de José Coronel Urtecho, Joaquín Pasos Argüello, Pablo Antonio y Manolo Cuadra, así como Luis Alberto Cabrales.

de papá / se abre con la llave de fá / con con llave de ré, / yo no sé. / El pueta / Yo la abriré / con una P. / (pausa) / Yo quiero tu dinero. / Fifí / Y yo te quiero / como papá a su bolero".

La teatralización de la unión fallida entre el poder mercantil y el arte señala, más que una tensión entre una oligarquía conservadora y una burguesía emergente[5], una tensión entre los intereses materialistas y la base católica de la oligarquía granadina a la que pertenecieron los integrantes de la Anti-academia[6]. En la década de 1930 un influyente sector de la sociedad y élite granadina que antiguamente había defendido los valores cosmopolitas y modernizantes de finales del siglo XIX asociados con la burguesía y el pensamiento liberal se empeñó en frenar el "oleaje de la inmoralidad" que a la vez relacionaron con las prácticas culturales y económicas impuestas por los intervencionistas estadounidenses. La clase oligárquica estaba siendo desplazada por los cambios económicos que habían producido la intervención estadounidense en Nicaragua, por el *dollar diplomacy* y el crack de 1929, así como el desplazamiento del partido Conservador de la administración y economía política nacional (Gobat 151). Los Antiacadémicos, por ende, no reprodujeron la misma dinámica de la vanguardia europea de una burguesía criticándose a sí misma sino constituyó el autoretrato de una oligarquía y una crítica del proyecto liberal del siglo XIX (representado por Darío) y la política estadounidense que en ese momento estaba desplazando el poder de esta oligarquía granadina[7].

---

[5] Michel Gobat señala que en Nicaragua fue la misma oligarquía granadina la que impulsó el desarrollo de la exportación del café a finales del siglo XIX, no una nueva clase media: "Contrary to conventional wisdom, then, the agroexport boom did not engender a new Liberal coffee bourgeoisie based in Managua and León, displacing a traditional, cattle-based Conservative oligarchy centered in Granada" (Gobat 57)

[6] Casi todos los miembros de la agrupación vivieron su infancia en Granada, asistieron al colegio jesuita Colegio Centro América y fueron hijos y nietos de ciudadanos afiliados al Partido Conservador (Arellano, *Entre la tradición* 44-45). Los miembros de la vanguardia nicaragüense también tuvieron lazos de parentesco.

[7] La postura anti-democrática y pro-corporativista del grupo vanguardista adoptó el modelo de dictadura corporativista católica de Primo de Rivera en España y de Salazar en Portugal; también recibió influencia de otros modelos de autoritarismo político-católico como el de Charles Maurrás y la Action Française, así como los Nacionalistas argentinos: "Nicaragua´s conservative oligarchs readily embraced Catholic, authoritarian corporatism largely

Don Chombón[8] y su familia, tal como el Ubu de Alfred Jarry,
no sólo representan personajes-tipos y caricaturas, sino también representan una parodia de todos los valores con los que la burguesía
se identifica. Fifí, por ejemplo, no representa la mujer e hija casta,
sino el materialismo y la lascivia. La escena catártica en donde se revelan los valores materialistas de la familia Chombón se da al final de
la obra. *Chinfonía* concluye con la muerte de todos los personajes por
la Muerte y su guadaña, no sin antes describir una escena patética que
revela la nimiedad de cada personaje: el Pueta suplica por más tiempo para escribir una obra maestra que, aunque le salga mal, lo inmor-
talizará; Doña Chomba quiere más tiempo para comer; Don Chombón le ofrece su esposa a la Muerte a cambio de él. En la escena final,
o a lo largo de la obra, cada personaje comete uno o varios de los
pecados capitales: lujuria, gula, pereza, avaricia, soberbia, ira y envidia.
Como Méndez de Penedo señala, la *Chinfonía* es una "moraleja cris-
tiana con ropaje bufo" que "pone en escena la derrota de la detestada
burguesía sin valores trascendentales a los cuales aferrarse, lo que
desenmascara su efímero poder terrenal" (*Teatro* 22).

Cuculcán, de Miguel Ángel Asturias, es la segunda obra de teatro
que señalaré, como teatro etnográfico rescata el legado precolombino[9]. Según Innes, el teatro vanguardista no sólo se caracterizó por

---

because its principles of organizing state-society relations closely corres-
ponded to those that underpinned their own antimodern vision of nation
and society. Not only did they valorize the organic view of hierarchically
ordered, harmonious, morally correct society that defined most contemporary versions of authoritarian corporatism, they also shared the social re-
formist and anticapitalist bent of Catholic corporatism. Further, conserva-
tives waging a moralizing crusade against U.S.-based visions of modernity
were attracted to Catholic corporatist regimes´ use of state to pursue moral
ends. Troubled by dollar diplomacy´s attack on their economic power, they
also came to embrace the corporatists´ vision that the state, not the free
market, should regulate the economy." (Gobat 224)

[8] Don Chombón, el burgués por excelencia, es retratado de modo similar al
famoso Ubu de Alfred Jarry porque se identifica por la caracterización gro-
tesca del burgués como glotón, gordo y materialista: "Saco mi alma del al-
mario, / mi alma de propietario millonario / y lentamente invento el inven-
tario / siguiente: / Tengo: / una spiroqueta pálida de abolengo, / un zancu-
do en mi escudo, / un higo en el ombligo. / Yo soy un tinajón con corazón,
/ un tinajón con saco y pantalón".

[9] A pesar de haberse publicado en la segunda edición de *Leyendas de Guatemala*, en 1948 (Buenos Aires, Ediciones Pleamar) fue escrita durante la tempo-

sus cualidades modernas, sino también en su "primitivismo" generado por dos facetas complementarias: "... the exploration of dream states or the instinctive and subconscious levels of the psyche; and the quasi-religious focus on myth and magic, which is the theatre leads to experiments with ritual and ritualistic patterning of performance" (2-3). *Cuculcán* ejemplifica estas dos vetas analíticas, ya que no sólo cuestiona los postulados de la realidad mediante su contraposición de lo masculino y femenino[10], sino también explora y rearticula mitos precolombinos mediante una estética moderna. Según Unruh, y comparto su visión, *Cuculcán* opera desde una postura diferente a la representación primitivista (presente en *Leyendas de Guatemala)*, ya que retrata el Nuevo Mundo como un "site of creative deception and critique" *(Double voicing* 527). Tal como en *Leyendas*, Asturias se inspira en un texto-base y lo modifica a su manera. Cuculcán, por ejemplo, es la versión latinizada del nombre Kukulkán, el dios patrón de las artes y las ciencias, el poeta, el gobernador justo, el hombre casto pero viril, en oposición a Tezcatlipoca/Huizilopotchli, el dios de la guerra, mañoso, destructor y sin principios que alude al mito tolteca de Kukulkán/Quetzalcoátl (Arias, *"Quetzalcoátl"* 631). El personaje Cuculcán no articula una voz narrativa, sino conforma uno

---

rada parisina asturiana (1924-1933); anterior a esta obra Asturias ya había experimentado con el teatro vanguardista en sus obras auto denominadas "fantomimas": *Rayito de Estrella* (1918-1928), *Émulo Lipolidón* (1929-1932) y *Aclasán* (1940-1942) (Méndez de Penedo, *Las fantomimas* 1225). El término "fantomima" conformó una nueva y sugerente palabra compuesta creada por las palabras "fantoche" y "pantomima", reflejo de la influencia lúdica vanguardista. Las fantomimas conforman breves piezas experimentales que fluctúan entre poesía y teatro, similares a los *sintesi* futuristas y anteceden al teatro en un acto de Ionesco por dos décadas. Estas primeras obras vanguardistas asturianas reflejan una toma de conciencia de la violencia fundacional de la nación latinoamericana plasmada en relaciones tensionadas entre los personajes femeninos y masculinos.
[10] En la obra se borran las diferencias entre el sol y la luna, el hombre y la mujer, cuando personajes como la Tortuga con flecos dice "El hombre es la mujer con todas las actividades del día. No hay otra diferencia" (349). Mientras que lo masculino, representado por el poder de Cuculcán y su imitador, Chinchibirín, establece el orden, lo femenino es representado como lo oscuro e irracional. Guacayamo le indica a Chinchibirín: "La mujer es la locura... (e)s el piquete de la tarántula...", la Tortuga Barbada dice, repetidamente, que las mujeres son metales en estado de algodón (349).

de los cuatro personajes principales de la obra. Los otros personajes son Yaí, la prometida de Cuculcán; Chinchibirín, un guerrero y vasallo de Cuculcán; Guacamayo, un pájaro multicolor asociado con la figura del autor; y el mismo rey-gobernador Cuculcán, se admite cierta polifonía textual.

Cuculcán, similar a otras obras vanguardistas como *Altazor*, refleja sintáctica y temáticamente una crisis referencial. Mediante una contraposición de opuestos, y utilizando el tropo del espejo, *Cuculcán* borra los límites entre un ente y el otro. El inicio del primer acto, Chinchibirín le informa a Cuculcán que el guardador de la selva "(e)stuvo entre los conejos y las frutas del papaya y vio que se cambiaban, que las frutas echábanse a correr como conejos, y se prendían a mamar en los papayos, como frutas, los conejos". Cuculcán constantemente repite "¡Soy como el Sol!", mientras que Guacamayo le responde "¡Eres el Sol, acucuác, tu palacio de forma circular, como el palacio del Sol, tiene cielos, tierras, estancias, mares, lagos, jardines para la mañana, para la tarde, para la noche; (lento, solemne) para la mañana, para la tarde, para la noche!...". El palacio de Cuculcán es descrito como una estructura circular que perpetúa la ciclicidad temporal, mientras que a Guacamayo se le confunde constantemente con un arcoíris, con el fuego y con otros tipos de aves. Guacamayo representa el juego verbal y la creatividad que no busca engañar intencionalmente: "Guacamayo con su lengua enredó a los dioses por los pies, al confundirles sus sandalias, al hacerles andar con los ecos del pie derecho en el pie izquierdo..." (356). Mientras que Cuculcán representa la referencialidad y continuidad ontológica, Guacamayo desestabiliza el referente y así genera una dinámica cíclica creadora.

La obra de teatro, *Cuculcán*, narra y escenifica cómo Yaí, junto con la ayuda de Guacamayo, logra persuadir a Cuculcán a cambiar el orden establecido en su reino. La narración gira en torno a dos ejes temáticos: la contraposición de dos mitos o sistemas de conocimiento relacionados al trayecto Solar y el mito de Yaí. En cuanto al primer eje, la segunda escena de la obra desarrolla la discusión entre Chinchibirín y Guacamayo en relación al trayecto solar: Chinchibirín cree en la teoría copernicana, Guacamayo establece que el trayecto solar durante el día es producto de un espejismo y que el sol realmente llega al cénit y regresa de donde sale. Otro debate trata del destino de Yaí quien, según Guacamayo, será asesinada en la madrugada, después de pasar la noche de bodas con Cuculcán, para impedir su descendencia. Guacamayo logra convencer a Chinchibirín de su amor por Yaí, impulsándolo a retar la autoridad de Cuculcán y a buscar a Yaí para hacerla su pareja. Ambos ejes revelan dos paradigmas o interpretaciones contrastantes.

Para convencer a Cuculcán de no asesinarla, Yaí accede a frotar sus manos-espejos creados por el aliento de Guacamayo en los cabellos de Cuculcán y emitir la palabra compuesta "girasol". Cuando ella hace esto Cuculcán pierde momentáneamente su orientación y luego dispersa sus sentidos a los cuatro puntos cardinales, sugiriendo un cambio paradigmático. Me interesa enfatizar aquí la importancia que Asturias le otorga a la palabra escrita y hablada, ya que Guacamayo y Yaí ("... una palabra con destino de molusco"), dos personajes asociados con la escritura, son los actantes de la trama. Si tomamos en cuenta la enunciación repetitiva que Guacamayo le hace a Chinchibirín, reconocemos que el único cambio proviene de la unión de estos tres personajes: "¡Tú, el arquero! ¡Tú, el arquero! ¡Yaí, la flecha! ¡Yaí, la flecha! Y yo, el acroiris... cuác, cuác, cuác, cuác... ¡El destino del Sol esta jugado!". Esta transformación, empero, no es absoluta porque un personaje femenino y diminuto que vive en una nube, Abuela de los Remiendos, frena la transformación y restablece un balance. Lo anterior lo sabemos porque la obra concluye con dos interpretaciones del evento: la de Blanco Aporreador de Tambores, que acusa a la mujer por su "crecido instinto", reproduciendo el discurso judeo-cristiano de la expulsión edénica; la segunda interpretación es la de la Tortuga Barbada quien dice: "...Yaí encendió una rosa en los cabellos del Sol, eso fue todo!". La sabiduría, simbolizada en un personaje femenino anciano, la "Abuelita de las Abuelas", salva el imperio de Cuculcán del cambio o desintegración total. Como dice Blanco Aporreador de Tambores: "...el mundo por tu aguja seguirá en la realidad y en los espejos, en los hombres, en las mujeres y en los guacamayos. Cada uno en su mundo, afuera, y todos reunidos en el espejo sonámbulo del sueño". Cuculcán se reintegra pero ya no es el mismo ya que se le encendió una rosa en los cabellos.

Si situamos esta obra de teatro asturiano históricamente, este cambio de orden puede interpretarse como la transición de la dictadura liberal de Estrada Cabrera a un sistema democrático-liberal, aunque breve, de la década de 1920. Similar a *Cucuclán*, cuya trinidad Chinchibirín/Yaí/Guacamayo, unión del guerrero, el artista y la palabra oral/psique, logra modificar el punto de vista de Cuculcán, en Guatemala la caída de la dictadura cabrerista se produjo por una alianza pasajera entre la élite capitalina con sectores populares obreros y artesanales, y una facción del ejército organizados alrededor del partido Unionista. Asturias vivió esta euforia momentánea antes de partir a París (experiencia que años después incluiría en *Viernes de Dolores*). Después de una serie de gobiernos militares se reinstauró de nuevo otra dictadura, la de Jorge Ubico, que duraría de 1931 a 1944.

Es importante señalar que el acercamiento académico de Asturias hacia el mundo y mitología precolombina se debe a la influencia de Georges Reynaud, director de Estudios sobre las Religiones de la América Precolombina en la Escuela de Altos Estudios de París. Asturias colaboró con Reynaud en la traducción del francés al español del libro sagrado de la cultura quiché, el *Popol Vuh*, y el de los cachiqueles, *Anales de los Xahil*, en 1927 y 1928 respectivamente (Méndez de Penedo, *Teatro* 1280). Es igualmente importante señalar que, como admite Mario Roberto Morales, hubo un viraje ideológico en la obra asturiana durante su estadía parisina, un abandono (aunque para muchos no integral) de la mentalidad oligárquica (presente en el ensayo de tesis *El problema social del indio*) hacia la adhesión de una mentalidad modernizante, así como un "operativo artístico literario de inclusión y fusión de las culturas subalternas indígenas a una versión transculturada y mestiza de la guatemalidad" (*Miguel Ángel Asturias: la estética y la política de la interculturalidad* 570). Como muestra de este giro asturiano, se debe tomar en consideración el artículo "Las posibilidades de un teatro americano", publicado el 18 de julio de 1932 (*Teatro*, Méndez de Penedo 839-843). Este es un texto programático que elabora una propuesta abierta para la creación de un nuevo teatro americano experimental (Méndez de Penedo, "Introducción" XXXV). "Las posibilidades" establece una relación intrínseca entre la producción cultural-teatral y la identidad americana de base precolombina. Asturias procura rescatar la tradición oral por medio de documentos y obras autóctonas como *Ollantay* (inca) y *Guerrero de Rabinal* (maya-quiché), así como obras sincréticas aún representadas como *El Mashimón*, que puede ser, según él, "desorientadores si no se les trata con precaución" (Méndez de Penedo, *Teatro* 839). Aún impera el peso de la tradición escrita sobre la oral. Esta práctica teatral, según Asturias, establecería un proceso gradual de autoconocimiento o desvelamiento ontológico que condujera la expresión cultural americana de un primer nivel infantil y lúdico a un segundo nivel de madurez. Percibiendo la exclusión de lo indígena como la base del problema americano, Asturias propuso el teatro como el medio idóneo para propiciar la concientización social y generar un modelo de identidad nacional simbólicamente anclado en el legado precolombino.

El teatro centroamericano vanguardista, a diferencia del teatro dadaísta, no buscó desarticular la expresión teatral ni la institución del arte, ya que el arte, a pesar de haberse distanciado de la política estatal, aún ejercía legitimación y autoridad social. Como postula Pelletieri, el teatro latinoamericano de la década de 1920 fue reformador y difirió del teatro iconoclasta europeo porque no buscó desarticular la función o institucionalidad del teatro; más que "vanguardista" este teatro fue "modernizador" (638)[11]. Ambas obras de teatro que analizo en este trabajo apoyan esta concepción de una vanguardia reformista, ya que en ellas se escenifican – de diferentes focalizaciones no hegemónicas – dos comunidades imaginadas o modelos de la nación moderna y el lugar del artista en estos ámbitos deseados, no se intentan socavar ni la institución del arte ni la nación.

He intentado dar una breve interpretación y comparación entre dos obras de teatro de la vanguardia histórica centroamericana con la finalidad de exponer dos distintos modos en que se inscriben, desde una nueva estética, distintas versiones de comunidades deseadas. Un complemento necesario a este trabajo es la investigación de la recepción de estas dos obras de teatro. La constante presencia e influencia de Miguel Ángel Asturias en el ámbito político y cultural guatemalteco, así como el de José Coronel Urtecho y Joaquín Pasos en el nicaragüense hace el estudio de esta obra vanguardista un elemento esencial en el estudio de la construcción (y exclusión) de la identidad centroamericana y su historiografía literaria.

---

[11] Pellettieri asevera que existen dos fases del teatro de la modernización latinoamericana: el primer período que abarca de 1920 a 1960 y el segundo que parte de 1950-60 en adelante. Este erre al asumir que la primera fase constituyó una postura imitativa de las influencias europeas y norteamericanas así como un rechazo de la tradición teatral latinoamericana previa, mientras que la segunda representa la producción teatral nacionalizada.

Bibliografía

Arellano, Jorge Eduardo. *Entre la tradición y la modernidad : el movimiento nicaragüense de vanguardia.* Serie Literaria. San José, Costa Rica: Libro Libre, 1992.

Arias, Arturo. "Quetzalcóatl, la hibridación y la identidad indígena: *Leyendas de Guatemala* como laboratorio étnico." *Miguel Ángel Asturias: cuentos y leyendas.* Ed. Morales, Mario Roberto. Colección Archivos. España: ALLCA XX, 2000.

Asturias, Miguel Ángel. *Miguel Ángel Asturias: Teatro* Colección Archivos Ed. Penedo, Lucrecia Méndez de. España: ALLCA XX, 2003.

Cardullo, Bert y Robert Knopf. *Theatre of the Avant-Garde, 1890-1950: A Critical Anthology* Ed. Cardullo, Bert and Robert Knopf. New Haven: Yale University Press, 2001.

Coronel Urtecho, José y Joaquín Pasos "Chinfonía Burguesa." *3 obras de teatro nuevo* Ed. Cuadra, Pablo Antonio. Nicaragua: Academia Nicaragüense de la Lengua 1957. 9-43.

Gobat, Michel. *Confronting the American Dream : Nicaragua under U.S. Imperial Rule.* American Encounters/Global Interactions. Durham: Duke University Press, 2005.

Innes, Christopher *Avant Garde Theatre: 1892-1992.* 1993. USA: Routledge, 1993.

Mendez de Penedo, Lucrecia. "Teatro vanguardista nicaragüense." *Centroamericana* 5 (1995): 9-25.

Méndez de Penedo, Lucrecia. "Introducción de la coordinadora." *Miguel Ángel Asturias: Teatro* Ed. Penedo, Lucrecia Méndez de. España: ALLCA XX, 2003. XXI-XLVIII.

Méndez de Penedo, Lucrecia. "Las fantomimas barrocas y sombrías de Miguel Ángel Asturias." *Miguel Ángel Asturias: Teatro.* Ed. Méndez de Penedo, Lucrecia. Francia: ALLCA XX, 2003. 1225-33.

Morales, Mario Roberto. "Miguel Ángel Asturias: la estética y la política de la interculturalidad." *Miguel Ángel Asturias: cuentos y leyendas* Ed. Morales, Mario Roberto. 1era Ed. ed. Colección Archivos. España ALLCA XX, 2000. 553-607.

Pelletieri, Osvaldo. "Teatro latinoamericano de los veinte: una práctica teatral modernizadora." *Revista Iberoamericana* Vol. LVII.Num. 155-156 (1991): 635-42.

Puchner, Martin. *Poetry of the Revolution : Marx, Manifestos, and the Avant-Gardes*. Translation/Transnation. Princeton: Princeton University Press, 2006.

Unruh, Vicky. "The Chinfonia Burguesa: A Linguistic Manifesto of Nicaragua's Avant-Garde " *Latin American Theatre Review* 1987 (1987): 37-48.

---. *Latin American Vanguards : The Art of Contentious Encounters*. Latin American Literature and Culture. Berkeley: University of California Press, 1994.

Videla de Rivero, Gloria. *Direcciones del vanguardismo hispanoamericano : estudios sobre poesía de vanguardia en la década del veinte : documentos*. Biblioteca De América. Pittsburgh, Pa.: Instituto Internacional de Literatura Iberoamericana, 1994.

BODY, IDENTITY, AND THE WRITING PROCESS IN THE NARRATIVE OF CARMEN BOULLOSA

Jessica Burke

Contemporary Mexican author Carmen Boullosa is a dedicated and prolific writer. She has published seventeen novels to date, not to mention her theater, poetry, short stories, essays and other artistic endeavors. Through a fragmented discourse that reflects her characters' fragmented notions of self, Boullosa creates parodic, self-reflective novels that center in a plot but also engage with their own creation as texts and the practice of story-telling as an art. The particular and personal "histories" that she creates in her novels dialogue with and question the official History that often has excluded or silenced certain voices. Boullosa gives these marginalized groups a voice and a space from which they can express themselves. The physical body and the "body" of the text are both works in progress, requiring the active participation of the reader in the construction of their meaning. Boullosa's narrators struggle to define themselves under the pressure of expectations put forth by both society and the novelistic genre itself. By exploring the relationship between characters' bodies, their sense of self, and the text that contains them, my research shows how Boullosa's fragmented narrative allows for reconfiguration of physical and textual bodies, and of identity. It is through dismantling instituted notions of gender, identity, body, and narrative that Boullosa creates a space for reinvention of the self, and of novelistic form.

Boullosa's texts are not as widely read as those of her more mainstream contemporaries, perhaps due to their complexity and lack of narrative "flow." Critics situate Boullosa's writing within postmodern debates due to its self-reflective, fragmentary and often parodic nature. In several of her narratives, Boullosa inserts herself into the text as "the author," a literary projection of Carmen Boullosa which in essence becomes another character in the text. Sometimes referring to herself as "Carmen" or "Boullosa" and at others as "la autora" she subjects herself to the questioning and even ridicule of her own characters and narrators.

Regardless of who is narrating, the narrator maintains an intimate connection with his/her perceived audience. The reader is always kept close, whether directly invoked in the text or not. At times it seems that Boullosa's narrators rely on the reader more than the reader can rely on the narrators, which creates an interesting dynamic in terms of reader response. Titling her work with such disclaimers as "Ingobernable," "Teatro herético" or "Papeles irresponsables," Boullosa's intent often seems that of disconcerting the reader, calling into question the expectations that s/he brings to a text. The reader is taken on an imaginative adventure with multiple sidetrips, and sometimes the narrative path falls back on itself. We cannot expect a linear progression of plot or a traditional and reliable narrator who will guide us to a "natural" conclusion of the storyline, but we *can* expect to form an integral part of the meaning of the novel itself, as its readers, since it is through the reader that the text gains meaning. While the reader may be directly incorporated into Boullosa's texts, the metafictitious nature of the narrative will not allow us to stay there, caught up in the "story." The self-aware text needs a reader in order to construct itself as a narration, yet it demands a critical reader who will never forget the creative, inventive process at hand.

Boullosa's characters and narrators are subjects who have been marginalized by traditional literary and historical narrative; they are women, children, immigrants, natives, gypsies, prostitutes, pirates, slaves, vampires, cannibals, and ghosts. Instead of providing "types" to be assimilated into a certain historical framework, Boullosa's protagonists "break the mold," so to speak, with their complex and often hybrid nature. Their marginal position in society does not prohibit their right to a voice in Boullosa's texts, but rather allows them to provide alternative testimonies to the main "story" of History. These shadowy marginal spaces grant Boullosa's narrators a certain narrative freedom. They are not responsible for telling the Story of a Nation; they are simply telling *their* stories. These voices, however, are frequently broken ones, torn in their attempt to represent and pulled in different directions by social and narrative pressures. The narrators struggle with their sense of autonomy and identity, and through them is revealed the author's struggle with the autonomy and identity of her text.

The plurality of narrators and perspectives in Boullosa's texts are a testimony to her resistance to adopting one monolithic version of any historical event or figure. For example, it is the obsession with creating a "true" history of Moctezuma that stalls the many narratives that compose *Llanto: novelas imposibles*. Inspired to write about the famous Aztec emperor, each of the writers must abandon his/her attempt after realizing that creating a "true" history of Moctezuma is impossible. The multiple voices found in *Llanto: novelas imposibles* each offer a different version of the life and death of Moctezuma, truncated by the inability to continue. The resulting text--Boullosa's text--is the compilation of several "impossible" novels. Thus the only "possible" novel about Moctezuma is one that narrates the impossibility of accurately representing him. Boullosa's own resurrection of Moctezuma as a novelistic character dissolves into thin air at the end of the novel, unable to maintain a corporeal form in modern-day Mexico.

Faced with the impossibility of a cohesive "true story," we are forced to treat all perspectives as equally valid, thus contesting the grand "totalizing" historical narratives of the past. Such monolithic narrations that situate all events within their proper context do indeed presume a certain "sense" to be made of the information at hand. It is this "narrative" aspect of history that concerns Boullosa, a concern shared by many of her contemporaries. A recent collection of contemporary Mexican poetry (2002) entitled *Reversible Monuments* takes its name from a poem by Octavio Paz which contains within itself multiple ways to read and interpret its meaning. In his introduction, Eliot Weinberger concludes, "here then are Mexicos." The "Mexicos" present in Boullosa's work should perhaps be read as one writer's attempt to reverse certain Mexican monuments, whether they are the literary "monuments" of Mexican narrative, or the monumental pillars of Mexican society (the family, the church, the state).

The social and literary movements of the 1960s and 70s in Mexico had displayed a resistance to the myth of a unified nation with one Mexican "identity." Boullosa's narrative responds to this myth by blurring, erasing or transcending borders of gender and nation. Her novels set in the colony manage to reposition colonial narrative within a creative framework, providing new readings of Mexico and its past. However, this "reversal of monuments" through fiction extends beyond Mexico to address "monuments" of other parts of the world, revealing a vision with a much wider scope than traditional "national" or "regional" literature.

Boullosa's fragmented narrative is the result of careful readings of literary and historical texts. Her novels set in colonial times were inspired by sixteenth and seventeenth century accounts of the Conquest and colonization, and her first two novels, both set in childhood, were inspired by memories and journals that Carmen kept as a child. Boullosa's consultations of these historical and personal documents revealed inconsistencies, contradictions, and gaps, all of which contribute to the fragmentary nature of her novels, which openly acknowledge *their own* inconsistencies, contradictions, and gaps. What we know as reality is mapped out through a process of recollection, interpretation and postulation, a process limited by language and memory. In Boullosa's narrative, the gaps in memory and knowledge are either filled with imaginative invention or left glaringly open, revealing the absence of a monolithic "truth" (personal or historical) that would unite the various fragments of the text.

While Boullosa's work indubitably questions history as a narrative, it does not deny history as its source and inspiration. At the end of *La virgen y el violín*, Boullosa includes a note that details how she discovered the Italian painter Sofonisba Anguissola and was inspired to write her story. By mixing biographical information with her own imagination, Boullosa creates a love story where there was none (of record) and peppers her text with sub-plots that open up the world of the Italian Renaissance to include figures she imagines to be central to sixteenth century European society, even if they are marginal in the artistic representation of the era. The workshop belonging to Sofonisba's neighbor is full of artisans from diverse backgrounds, in terms of their nationality, religion and ethnicity. Magdalena, the African singer/dancer that Boullosa invented, is given voice and a space from which to tell her story. While tangential to the ill-fated love story that forms the axis of *La virgen y el violín*, Magdalena's songs and personal testimony are transcribed and given a place in this creative "historical" novel, connecting the central characters to the larger world and expanding their cultural context.

Boullosa again returns to the impossibility of knowing the "real" past in *De un salto descabalga la reina*, a novel loosely based on the Egyptian queen Cleopatra. Diómedes--Cleopatra's scribe and the novel's narrator--insists that he "almost" captures Cleopatra's true testimony but he is challenged by both external and internal obstacles. A fictitious history of Cleopatra, *De un salto descabalga la reina* doesn't come close to being a "historical" novel in the traditional sense. Although it includes historical events and figures, it also includes Cleopatra's abduction by a mythical bull that carries her across the sea and deposits her on the shore of the land of the Amazon women. This highly eroticized, imaginative history of Cleopatra does not seek to paint a historical portrait of the woman, but rather to create a very human, intimate, creative and sensual character who *could* have been Cleopatra and who is just as "real" as any other textual projection of the Egyptian queen.

Narrated by the man who betrayed her, the novel lends voice to Cleopatra, but always through a filter. She dictates her testimony to her scribe Diómedes, but he admits that he edits it as he sees fit, cutting out sentences that seem incoherent to him (31). He also confesses that the words that he attributes to Cleopatra are altered by Roman power. Diómedes vows to try again to capture Cleopatra's true testimony, but repeatedly fails: "Casi, casi, casi... Casi hablaba así, como aquí he anotado, casi fueron así sus palabras, o casi lo serían... si no fuera porque Cleopatra me dijo unas muy otras" (109). The scribe's struggle to capture the true essence of Cleopatra mirrors Boullosa's own literary project. While she does not pretend to represent the "real" Cleopatra, her text does engage with others which *have* made this attempt. By having her narrator openly acknowledge the influences on him which affect his narration, Boullosa reminds us that no writing takes place in a vacuum, and every writer is influenced by social, political, historical, cultural, linguistic and literary factors which shape how and what s/he writes.

Boullosa's novels engage with writing as a profession, as a passion, as a struggle, and as a creative outlet. Torn between his desire to create the perfect novel and his laziness when it comes to actually writing it, Vértiz, the protagonist of *La novela perfecta*, seems to have found the perfect solution when his neighbor, Lederer, approaches him with a new invention which will allow the writer to *imagine* his novel and record it without the use of words, by means of a sensor placed under the writer's tongue. The images from the writer's imagination are projected into the space of the laboratory where they take on lifelike qualities that far surpass those of any "written" novelistic character. Nevertheless, the writer is distracted by tangential stories, his own lack of focus, and his jealous suspicion of Lederer's intentions, both with the writer's novel, and with his wife. The partial "novel" made possible by Lederer's invention lacks structure and discipline, and eventually runs amok. A machine malfunction renders its characters discombobulated, fragmented, and creates a whirl of images and objects in the laboratory that ultimately kill the machine's creator, along with the possibility of creating a "perfect novel."

La novela perfecta was inspired by Boullosa's reading of Jorge Luis Borges and Adolfo Bioy Casares as a youngster. While her novel certainly echoes the style of fantastic literature, it also pokes fun at the writing profession and the literary marketplace. Driven by economic gain, the protagonist of *La novela perfecta* is initially delighted that he can create a novel without wrestling with language and the proper form. If Vértiz's "perfect novel" had ever been finished and reached a "reading" public, its "readers" would have experienced the novel *exactly* as its creator did. The reader would see, hear, even smell the characters, leaving little room to imagine them as s/he does with characters on the written page. One can see how Vértiz's "virtual" novel, on the brink of perfection, might be attractive to Boullosa and a slew of other writers, as opening the door to a new type of novel. Yet Lederer's marvelous invention is destined to fail, unable to contain the images produced by the writer's unbridled imagination, revealing how easily the creative project can get out of hand if imagination is the only element in the "writing" process. Lacking structure and discipline, the potentially "perfect" novel spirals out of control, coming to a violent, chaotic and abrupt end. Like *Llanto: novelas imposibles*, we are left with a novel that narrates the impossibility of producing the desired narrative.

Boullosa's narrative frequently has a sinister undercurrent that questions the humanity of the world we have created for ourselves. The violent, destructive tendencies of human beings toward themselves and toward each other is a central preoccupation of Boullosa's work. The fragmented body becomes a metaphor for fragmented society, unable to form a cohesive, harmonious whole. *Cielos de la tierra*, *La novela perfecta* and *El complot de los Románticos* all end with characters physically dismembering themselves. In *Cielos de la tierra*, this dismemberment follows the futuristic society's abolition of language and memory, suggesting a general deterioration of the social fabric. In the case of *El complot de los Románticos*, it is dead authors who are able to detach their body parts in order to hurl them at each other in a skirmish over the winning novel at a literary convention. The dismemberment of Boullosa's characters is always accompanied by chaos, and the end to a utopian dream. In *Powers of Horror*, Julia Kristeva asserts,

> On close inspection, all literature is probably a version of the apocalypse that seems to be rooted, no matter what its socio-historical conditions might be, on the fragile border (borderline cases) where identities (subject/object, etc.) do not exist or only barely so--double, fuzzy, heterogeneous, animal, metamorphosed, altered, abject. (207)

She continues, "Does one write under any other condition than being possessed by abjection, in an indefinite catharsis?" (208) Boullosa writes from the space described by Kristeva--a border space, where identities are "fuzzy," malleable, uncomfortable, and "abject." From the problematic nature of sexual identity during adolescence (a time of rapidly changing bodies) to the equally problematic nature of national identity during the time of the colony, Boullosa's characters and narrators constantly confront challenges to their notions of self. They are haunted by the ghosts of the past, whose phantasmagoric voices intrude upon their narration and make claims on the text itself. The past is inseparable from present reality. Thus the motivation to write reflects not only abjection and catharsis but also a desire to exorcise our internalized ghosts of the past--whether a personal past or the history of a nation.

Boullosa's protagonists--marginalized by history and traditional narrative--find in her fiction a space in which to redefine their place in society. Fearing the "Other" they are simultaneously drawn to it, while constantly seeking an identity that is "other"--one that might represent them in all of their complexity. Torn between the past and the present, plagued by fears and doubt, they turn to the text as a place to leave testimony of their struggle, as a record of their experience. Boullosa's narrators cling to the narrative process and to the reader in order to escape dissolution. The text is their one hope for immortality.

The question of transition is central to the physical, metaphorical and textual bodies of Boullosa's narrative. Her characters are morphing, changing, growing. Their identities are works in progress, even as the novels conclude. Likewise, the text itself is a work in progress, requiring the active participation of the reader as interpreter, participant and witness. Postmodern "identity" is constantly shape-shifting, resisting any kind of stasis or fixed definition; it is in constant transition. In Boullosa's texts, the body--as a metaphor for social identity--must necessarily be in the same fluctuating state of transition. The minute it stands still, it runs the risk of being captured and labeled by those who would reduce it to a "type." The body becomes the site of a re-negotiating of social identity. As "identity" of any kind is a social construct, Boullosa posits the body itself as a construct that can be manipulated, fragmented, transformed, and re-articulated in new ways. The fragmentation of physical bodies within the larger fragmented textual body of the novel is what allows Boullosa's characters and narrators to reconfigure themselves as they

see fit. There is freedom in the fragmented narrative; the space between the fragments is a space for the possible, and sometimes for
the impossible. Within a literary production that is as diverse as it is
extensive, the intimate relationship between body, identity and the
writing process is at the core of the creative (and destructive) narrative of Carmen Boullosa.

Works Cited

Boullosa, Carmen. *Antes.* México, D.F.: Punto de lectura, 1989.
---. *Cielos de la Tierra.* México, D.F.: Alfaguara, 1997.
---. *De un salto descabalga la reina.* México, D.F.: Editorial Debate, 2002.
---. *Duerme.* Madrid: Alfaguara, 1994.
---. *El complot de los románticos.* Madrid: Ediciones Siruela, 2009.
---. *El médico de los piratas.* Madrid: Ediciones Siruela, 1992.
---. *El velázquez de París.* Madrid: Ediciones Siruela, 2007.
---. "Isabel." *Prosa rota.* México, D.F.: Plaza & Janés, 2000.
---. *La Milagrosa.* México, D.F.: Ediciones Era, 1993.
---. *La novela perfecta.* México, D.F.: Alfaguara, 2006.
---. *La otra mano de Lepanto.* México, D.F.: Fondo de Cultura Econó-
mica, 2005.
---. *La virgen y el violín.* Madrid: Ediciones Siruela, 2008.
---. *Llanto: Novelas imposibles.* México, D.F.: Ediciones Era, 1992.
---. *Son vacas, somos puercos: filibusteros del mar Caribe.* México,
D.F.: Ediciones Era, 1991.
---. *Treinta años.* México, D.F.: Alfaguara, 1999.
De la torre, Mónica, and Michael Wiegers, eds. *Reversible Monuments:
Contemporary Mexican Poetry.* Port Townsend, WA: Copper Can-
yon Press, 2002.
D'Lugo, Carol Clark. *The Fragmented Novel in Mexico: the politics of form.*
Austin, TX: U of Texas P, 1997.
Dröscher, Barbara and Carlos Rincón, eds. and introd. Acercamien-
tos a Carmen Boullosa: Actas del Simposio "Conjugarse en infi-
nitivo-la escritora Carmen Boullosa." Berlin, Germany: Frey,
1999.
Kristeva, Julia. *Powers of horror: an essay on abjection.* Translated by Leon
S. Roudiez. New York: Columbia UP, 1982.

THE LITERATURE OF TERROR: SADUR'S GOTHIC-FANTASTIC FICTIONS

Tatyana Novikov

The introduction of the Gothic in Russia followed closely the historical period in which the Gothic flourished in England and Germany, namely, the late 18th and early 19th centuries. Ann Radcliffe's novels, in particular, were, for a time, very popular in Russia. In his book, *The Russian Gothic Novel and Its British Antecedents*, Mark Simpson makes a case that Russia proved to be a congenial home for the Gothic: the landscape provided a fitting background, both in the wild and gloomy regions of the mysterious north, and among the urban tenements of Russian cities, with their dark, winding streets and dilapidated staircases. The city was thus recognized as the cosmopolitan equivalent of the sinister spaces of older Gothic fiction. This setting, along with a preference for the emotional apprehension of reality, contributed to creating an atmosphere, in which the Gothic could easily take root. Discussing the origins of the Russian Gothic canon, Neil Cornwell writes: "A certain input from folklore, and such further native medieval ingredients as chronicles and saints' lives apart, Russian Gothic can be said to derive from an amalgam of European influences: the English Gothic novel, the tales of Hoffmann and the various schools of European idealistic and esoteric thought" (4). The critic associates the Gothic movement in Russia with the names of Karamzin, Marlinskii, Gnedich and Odoevsky. He also identifies Gothic elements in Gogol's *Vii* and *The Nose*, Dostoevsky's *The Brothers Karamazov*, Pushkin's *The Queen of Spades* and Lermontov's *Demon*.

Readers of Gothic fiction will recognize close affinities with the master of the Russian Gothic tale and a major figure of contemporary Russian prose, Nina Sadur, whose fiction in the Gothic mode is now coming to the forefront of the Russian Gothic canon. Some of her most striking work can be found in her stories and plays. Grounded in the demonic, the ghostly, and the supernatural, Sadur's writings synthesize these Gothic elements with the drive to define a culture in crisis during the post-Soviet era. They attempt to articulate collective anxieties about the integrity of the nation and the dissolution of order, meaning and identity. Sadur's figures represent cultural anxieties and give them fearful forms as demons, ghosts, and monsters, whose intrusion in the everyday life terrifies normality and undermines ordered notions of civilized humanity. The author offers a vision of a dark universe, where evil is unpredictable, ambivalence and uncertainty obscure single meaning, and Gothic excesses blur boundaries of fantasy and reality, while pandemonium underlies the surface of everyday life. Sadur's writings display a recognizable Gothic atmosphere, stock features and Gothic character types: inscrutable villains, menaced maidens, intense nocturnal scenes, sinister victimization, magical effects, haunted houses, and fascination with the otherworldly. However, with all their Gothic trappings, her narratives take place against an everyday Russian background. Sadur's settings allow her to create a landscape of fear and horror. The classic chronotope of the Gothic castle is replaced by its modern equivalent, the apartment. The most familiar of spaces, home, is associated with terror and presented as the scene of cruelties, violence, and sadistic acts.

The ghost story "The Blue Hand" uses the powerful Gothic formula of the maiden persecuted by a compulsive sadist. Dramatizing the inexplicable human urge to hurt others, it concerns a female villain, Maria Ivanovna, who inflicts steady, systematic cruelty upon Valia, her vulnerable neighbor in a communal apartment. In every way, Maria Ivanovna is a despicable character, small-minded, truly abusive, and vulgar, feared not only by Valia but also by her own family. Curiously, Maria's physicality is somehow masculine: her size makes her uninhibited by Russian cultural codes of submissive femininity; she is also a tough dominant wife who controls her husband with a firm and heavy hand.

The story records numerous incidents of grotesque abuse, as Valia is the frequent target of Maria's insulting comments. We are told that Maria "addressed Valia in an arrogant, brutish and insolent manner, waiting for Valia to talk back," trying to provoke her to "yell at the top of her lungs." But, frightened and humiliated, Valia "silently pressed against the wall" not knowing "how to handle Maria Ivanovna" or "how to shout back" (86, 87). Portrayed as a victim, Valia is subjected to constant psychological torment and violation of her personal boundaries. For example, Maria harasses Valia by eavesdropping when she has male company: "Maria Ivanovna started to groan in her own room, plunged into the hallway, her eyes popping out, and sat down on the communal chair – to eavesdrop, even if there was a movie showing on TV or she herself had company, she gave everything up for Valia, for her amorous sobs behind the thin dirty wall" (86, 87). The enthusiasm with which she harasses Valia resembles sadistic sexual pleasure.

Interestingly, the question of Maria's own victimization is also articulated in the story; she is depicted not only as the perpetrator of evil but also a victim of external pressures that drive her to violent behavior. Sadur reveals her angry history of serving time in prison. Harmed, if not actually destroyed by the brutal environment, Maria is driven by hatred for anyone who was never in jail, and assaulting Valia constitutes a safe way of rescuing her endangered sense of self. The text makes clear other roots of Maria's aggression: fear of advancing age, poverty, sexual frustration, and an existence saturated with boredom.

Crippled physically and emotionally as the violence intensifies, Valia is on the verge of breakdown. Maria's habitual displays of anger trigger Valia's attacks of migraines, when her "hands go numb and turn pale, almost blue" (87). Her identity as a victim reflects on her sexuality: her love life stops and bunches of warts grow on her left eyelid, her lip, and her chin, making Valia repellent. To shield herself from victimization, Valia withdraws into her dreams and empowers herself by imagining her tormentor violated in every possible way: "Maria Ivanovna is hanged in a prison yard with an alarming roll of drums in the background; her rectum falls out ...while Maria Ivanovna is taken down, brought back to life ... and after she opens her eyes, they make her stand up, bury her rectum and then they hang her again" (87). Such fantasy subversion of Maria's power is Valia's way of self-preservation.

Sadur's haunted universe is characterized by retributive justice. Death is inflicted on villainous Maria Ivanovna, not by the efforts of human justice, but through the intervention of Valia's own ghost. In a brief, sharply focused scene, we witness Maria's death by suffocation, and the story presents this act as a successful resolution of the violence and cruelties that dominated the text. Recalling Valia affected with migraine, the murder scene includes the magic image of "the blue hand" which can be seen as the otherworldly force avenging victimization:

> The hand grabbed her chubby throat and started choking her. Maria Ivanovna began to wheeze, waving her fingers trying to get away, but the hand squeezed harder and harder until funeral lights swam before her eyes. (88)

This Gothic scene leaves us off balance. Other than assuming that Valia turned into a witch, we cannot account for the appearance of the blue hand and it continues to haunt us. The story becomes even more fantastic with Valia's mysterious disappearance and the fact that her nightgown crumbles into dirt at first touch. While our imaginations are left to ponder this enigmatic ending, we feel pleasure at these magic occurrences. Affirming the possibility of miracles, the story refuses closure, and because its supernatural events remain unexplained, it creates an atmosphere that is both familiar and strange.

Exploring the dynamics of villainy and victimization, other stories portray traumatized characters terrified by events beyond human knowledge and control. Fear and horror are major themes in "The Little Redhead," where supernatural events, magnified by a haunted environment, dark and obscure setting and tempestuous atmosphere, help build the story's eerie quality. Sadur leads us into a nightmarish world in which the virtuous, distressed and menaced young heroine Natasha lives in a spooky apartment that harbors mystery and gloom. Her landlady, an old sinister woman, supposedly, a witch and a distinctly Gothic figure, relentlessly harasses Natasha. In addition, this fearsome shamanistic woman is regularly visited by supernatural spectral figures, whose ghostly voices cause Natasha's mounting terror: "And every night someone squeaked in the old woman's room. The old woman quarreled or consulted with these squeaking voices. And Natasha was dying of fear every night" (65).

In a characteristic Gothic fashion, Natasha is pursued by the power of evil. This pyrotechnic tale of the heroine's recurring nocturnal meetings with a supernatural visitant, the little redhead monster of the title, is Gothic in its imagery and evocation of claustrophobic terror during Natasha's ordeals. All the Gothic machinery is here – gusts of wind, terrible sounds behind the door, screams of blood curling intensity, strange shadows, and spectral footprints, as well as the feeling of a malevolent will at work. We find an instance of genuine Gothic horror, when Natasha lies sweating with terror as the sinister fantastic being whispers at the victim's bedside:

> And all over again: the voices start squeaking, the old woman squabbling, the curtain dancing and Natasha is trembling under the blanket. She covers herself up from head to toe and holds her breath. Suddenly, she hears someone run up

and stand by. She can feel him, but, frightened, is unable even to cry. (67)

It is important to recognize that Sadur's character rejects conventional passivity of the Gothic heroine and learns to avoid the intense dread by taking sedatives before going to bed and sleeping through the nightly terrifying experiences. Eventually, the story affords Natasha a happy ending, when she is saved by a socially acceptable hero, typically reserved for the Gothic heroine. Thus, consistent with the Gothic plotting, she receives a marriage proposal from a fellow-student and leaves the haunted apartment.

Sadur's short play "Red Paradise" stands as her most significant creation in Gothicism and as such warrants extended consideration. This classic piece of Gothic writing uses and transforms the stock Gothic types of the virtuous heroine and the villain hero. The author creates a marginalized figure of Taisa, a freakish character and a passive docile woman, who has suffered physical and psychological abuse from two local men, Tolia and Volodia. The two emerge as pure emblems of evil beyond redemption. Among other things, we learn that the men "chased Taisa in their truck, knocking her down." They call her "stupid," "bitch" and even conspire to murder Taisa, since "society will only be grateful if we bump off this idiot" (273).

Sadur's play contains many of the standard props of the Gothic writing. At its center stands what has been described as the major locus of Gothic plots, the decaying castle. The 9th century Genoa Fortress is a large building with towers, narrow passages and a chamber equipped with grilled windows and ancient weaponry – swords, spears, armor, helmets and instruments of torture. Pervaded by an atmosphere of gloom and threat, the fortress stands on a massive cliff. There are sounds of waves pounding on the rocks below.

Lured by Taisa, the two men set off to the fortress in search of a buried treasure. The fearsome structure turns out to be a House of Horrors, where submissive Taisa suddenly metamorphoses into an aggressive predator who wreaks devastation among the men. Taisa now possesses a mythic and terrifying force, holding absolute power over them. Her meekness turns into cruelty, and she becomes a maniac, blood-thirsty and savage. As Taisa abandons her victim status, her suppressed rage is vented and her long-kept frustration distills into hatred. Tolia and Volodia, too, are subject to strange transformations, as Sadur deconstructs the all-powerful, authoritative and sinister villain types. The two males react with horror and despair facing the monster woman who now displays uncharacteristic ferociousness, aggression and lust for power.

As is commonly known, the defining feature of the Gothic is a persecuted heroine fleeing or trapped inside a castle. (We have seen such heroines, confined within sinister apartments, in Sadur's stories). In contrast, "Red Paradise" places menaced males within the ancient fortress, where they are caught in a labyrinth of darkness and are pursued and violated by a sadistic woman, who bears the richest affinities to compulsive Gothic villains. The fortress takes on a clearly Gothic role as the seat of medieval barbarism, while Taisa conforms to the Gothic stereotype of the tyrannical master of a feudal castle.

The play becomes a grotesque bloody messy affair as Tolia and Volodia are tortured and repeatedly murdered in the most resourceful ways and then brought back to life so that this orgy of violence and degradation could continue. Tolia and Volodia turn into emasculated and horrified creatures; attacked by Taisa, they lie passive and still, waiting to be tortured by the blood-thirsty monster-woman - a complete opposite of the view that it is the hapless Gothic heroine who is to embody the patriarchal concept "suffer and be still." In this striking reversal, the two men are transformed into objects of oppression, displacing the conventional Gothic villain-hero. Indeed, in her systematic killing and sadistic mutilation of the men, which includes grilling Volodia alive and eating his meat, well-seasoned with spices, Taisa appears to be an avenging agent for all past Gothic heroines. Critic De Jong insightfully notes that "truth and freedom are achieved through basic transgression" (49). Taisa's figure liberates explosive power, transgressive energies, rage and breaks down all kinds of stereotypes, boundaries, and behaviors. As the play's characters cross the boundaries between the masculine and the feminine, the living and the dead, all divisions are breached, all the rules and hierarchies turned upside down. Literary criticism has suggested that the Gothic must be understood as precisely this blurring of boundaries: "We have thus come to understand the Gothic as a spectacle of the mutual interpenetration of categories that social and ideological institutions have long been striven to keep separate" (Kavka, 211).

As noted, Sadur's writing contains supernaturalism of the Gothic sort presenting the reader with a mysterious universe beyond understanding, with supernatural agencies dictating the action. Its chief source of power is the tension between real happenings and the unexplainable, between the familiar and the unpredictable. Challenging the rational order and the bounds of possibility by sudden intrusions of supernatural events, Sadur forces us to reconsider the nature of the world.

Her story "Silky Hair" is a tale of witchcraft, black magic, and an awakening to the power of evil. In it, a grief-stricken mother learns that her sick son is under a spell of a shamanistic family friend, who holds the keys to his life in the form of a magic button. In quest of this magic object, the mother pursues her malicious friend, finds the button and, transforming into a murderous monster, destroys the woman's child. In Sadur's fictional world, people revert to barbarism with frightening rapidity. The story "Witch's Tear" relates another dark tale of a vindictive and ruthless heroine's murderous intentions towards her ex-lover: her obsessive desire to ruin him partakes of supernatural powers. But everything she plots against him redounds upon herself, including the young lady's fatal rendezvous with a witch and finally her death in the midst of a gloomy sinister Gothic landscape.

For Sadur, it is not enough that her narratives should enact the psychology of paranoia, represent the feminine self as threatened and speak to her fears; those fears are to be mysterious. To the very end there remains doubt and confusion, and the supernatural ambience keeps readers uncertain as to what is real. Countering certitude with anxiety and mystery, Sadur's art reflects a time when all certainty is destroyed.

Works Cited

Cornwell, Neil. "Russian Gothic: An Introduction." *The Gothic-Fantastic in Nineteenth-Century Russian Literature*. Ed. Neil Cornwell. Amsterdam-Atlanta: Rodopi B.V., 1999.

De Jong, A. *Nightmare Culture*. London: Secker and Warburg, 1973. Quoted in: Horner, Avril. "French Fiction and *Nightwood*." *European Gothic*. Ed. Avril Horner. Manchester and New York: Manchester University Press, 2002.

Kavka, Misha. "Gothic on Screen." *The Cambridge Companion to Gothic Fiction*. Ed. Jerrold E. Hogle. Cambridge: Cambridge University Press, 2002. 211.

Sadur, Nina. "Siniaia ruka" ("The Blue Hand"). Glazami zhenshchiny. Dajdzhest novoi russkoi literatury. Moscow: GLAS, 1994.

----. "Malen'kii, ryzhen'kii" ("The Little Redhead"). *Glazami zhenshchiny. Dajdzhest novoi russkoi literatury.* Moscow: GLAS, 1994.

----. "Krasnyi paradiz" ("Red Paradise"). *Obmorok.* Vologda: Poligrafist, 1999.

Simpson, Mark S. *The Russian Gothic Novel and Its British Antecedents.* Columbus, Ohio: Slavica, 1986.

THE MATERIALITY OF MIND IN STEFAN ZWEIG'S *CHESS STORY*

Terry Cochran

I

Literature, as an essential vehicle of the human imaginary, consists in far more than the projection of an unrealizable world, a view of some ideal past, or an unreal picture giving solace in times of crisis. Literature also constitutes a repository of human thinking, sometimes abstract, that goes well beyond strictly empirical questions or events taking place in the world of literary representation. In other words, what we call the literary is the written record of human thought that never makes itself wholly present, that remains inevitably potential, largely dependent on posterity to lay claim to the thought it conveys. These brief observations describe the context in which I would like to address a very particular concern lying at the heart of Stefan Zweig's enigmatic text best known in English under the title of "Chess Story." A great deal of pathos surrounds this short story or novella, in part because stems from the last weeks of Zweig's life, which ended tragically in suicide. In the months leading up to Zweig's death, in addition to "Chess Story," he worked on and completed two other important book projects, including a personal essay on Montaigne and his autobiography, *The World of Yesterday*. Retrospectively, these two books resonate deeply with what critics have called the "Jewish exile" (Goodwin 1), the historical context that provoked Zweig to take stock of his life before bringing it to an abrupt end. In studying Montaigne's *Essays* during this period, Zweig reflected on his own mortality in the face of unbounded despair, whereas his autobiographical writing, what one commentator calls Zweig's "testament spirituel" or "spiritual last will and testament" (Jaccard 8), sums up his past world as he saw it in that moment. But what of *Schachnovelle*, this novella in which the game of chess is proclaimed as a primary character? What was the nature of its urgency or, to put it differently, how might one describe its spiritual legacy?

II

Above and beyond its strangeness in this clutch of three posthumous books, the novella has an additional distinction in the context of Zweig's work: in the course of its narrative, it makes straightforward reference to events in contemporary history (that is, to Hitler); in particular, it evokes the psychological, physical, and legal forces that the SS state brought to bear in confiscating the property and wealth of the Jewish population and other real or imagined adversaries. Yet the history of the time simultaneously offers the backdrop for a much broader reflection on history and, more specifically, on the human mind as protagonist of that history. This story's elements have, of course, been subjected to numerous forms of narrative dissection, for its intricate structure of embedded or interlocking realities provides limitless fodder for literary criticism. This criticism has focused on the story's overall narrator who was traveling by ship from New York to Buenos Aires (mimicking Zweig's own voyages to South America in exile), the confrontation between two worldviews, two mindsets – embodied in the chess match between the uncultivated, even uncouth chess master Czentovic and Dr. B., a cultivated and somewhat high-strung passenger who seems to be a superb chess player – or the life story of the character known as Dr. B. who explains how his apparent proficiency in chess came about.

In what follows, I want to broach a fundamental aspect of this latter account - that is, Dr. B.'s narrative - that enjoys a special status in Zweig's novella; it portrays a coherent worldview that addresses one of the most crucial issues of human existence. In confiding his story to the narrator, most directly to clarify his seemingly uncanny abilities in the game of chess, Dr. B. offers a highly sophisticated interpretation of his experiences as a captive undergoing psychological torture at the hands of the Nazis. In this story within a story, the reader learns that Dr. B. owes his extraordinary chess abilities to having found a manual of famous chess matches that was his only reading material during the time he was held captive by the Gestapo. His intimate relationship to this manual, which constitutes the backbone of his account, also provokes the psychological incident as a prelude to his crisis in the story. As the doctor states, he read or studied this manual unceasingly until he came to subsume in his own singular mind two adversaries facing off over a chess board; not surprisingly, he became mentally distressed, losing control of his own conscious mind, becoming hospitalized after having severely wounded his hand by ramming it through a window. This interior struggle ends his forced confinement; besides his profound knowledge of chess and apparently fragile mental constitution, all that physically remains of this experience is the "deep scar" on his hand. In addition to bestowing a dramatic unity on diverse narrative threads, this account proves exemplary of more extensive reflection on the relationship between the human mind and historical continuity, about the nature of thinking and its transmission. The analysis that the Dr. undertakes in these pages makes recourse to very precise language, unlike what we so quickly associate with novelizing discourse, and closely resembles that of the philosophical treatise.

III

In a narrow historical perspective, this account proves striking in its sociopolitical awareness, which is even more accentuated today because of our greater knowledge of what was actually transpiring at that moment. Dr. B. begins the narrative about his personal captivity by stating that, contrary to what one might expect, he will not tell a concentration camp story [*vom Konzentrationslager erzählen*], but, being in another categorie [*Kategorie*], composed of those from whom the Nazis wanted information, he was destined for "special treatment" [*besondere Behandlung*], a term that, once again, has a resonance today that would have been inaudible at the time (Zweig 54-45). Zweig was writing in late 1941 and early 1942 (his suicide took place on February 22) and presumably knew little of Nazi extermination camps (the Wannsee Conference, which formalized the apparatus of extermination camps, took place only on January 20, 1942). The reference to concentration camps, though, was not gratuitous, for its negative example allowed for a more meticulous understanding of his imprisonment, its modalities and implications. The torture [*Folterung*] to which he was subjected was in no way physical [*körperlich*] but acted solely on the mind. There were not even any threats nor, apparently, perverse scenarios, as is so often the case in sophisticated psychological torture. Rather than executive violence, typically characteristic of the Gestapo, all aggression took place on a symbolic level, and the contours of this particular application of torture bear careful consideration. It is strangely described almost as a philosophical problem, along the lines of a thought experiment; while Dr. B. vigorously and even rigorously depicted the conditions to which he was subjected, the significance of what he underwent was interpreted in clinical fashion. For those in his "category," not bodily tied to the rack, the cultivation of nothingness was to produce the desired effects:

> Nothing was done to us; we were placed in complete noth-
> ingness [*Nichts*], for it is well known that no thing on earth
> puts so much pressure on the human soul [*die menschliche
> Seele*] as nothingness. In enclosing each one of us in a com-
> plete vacuum, in a room that was hermetically sealed off
> from the outside world, such pressure, coming from within
> rather than from without through beatings and cold, would
> finally open our mouths [or : force our lips open: *der uns
> schließlich die Lippen aufsprengte*]. (56)

This nothingness concerns a very specific relationship between the
interior and the exterior, between the inner mind or "soul" and the
external world, including, at least in theory, other human beings. This
relationship belongs intrinsically to human existence; we all participate in this dialectic between our own interiority and the external
material things that we create and to which we react. Our very consciousness is tied to this to-and-fro, to an ongoing engagement with
material objects or living subjects inhabiting the surrounding world,
offering themselves for our perusal and as interlocutors for our in-
cessant thinking that we then externalize.

What this story continually refers to as nothingness or emptiness signals the advent of a rupture between inner and outer, the
intentional creation of a barrier to hinder the passage between inside
and outside, between the inner mind and the external world. Yet,
contrary to what one might expect, the situation does not corre-
spond exactly to sensory deprivation as understood in the context of
a carefully controlled scientific experiment. In this instance, the individual tortured by the Nazi régime was not locked up in a dark room
but rather in a hotel room where nothing ever changed, with the
door barred and no view opening toward the exterior; as the character himself puts it:

> … I never heard a human voice; from morning to night,
> from night to morning, eyes, ears, all senses were deprived
> of even the most limited nourishment, leaving one desper-
> ately alone with one's body and four or five mute objects -
> table, bed, window, and washbasin. (57)

Being imprisoned, even if in a relatively anodyne hotel room, constitutes a real, physical constraint that is certainly unpleasant and, perhaps, life threatening, especially in the context of the SS state. At this
juncture, it is important to bear in mind that this account projects a

backdrop for sketching out a very specific understanding of history and the human mind. This dramatization compels the reader to imagine the ramifications of extreme solitude, the ensuing boredom and even, in this case, the onset of madness. As the story represents them, these circumstances create the vacuum, the nothingness surrounding Dr. B. and constituting the - in his view, very effective - means of torture.

Yet in the context of this portrayal, what is the nature of this seemingly innocuous sense deprivation? In this depiction, nothingness is more than a word or literary figure that simply conveys an imaginary; it is a concept in its own right and bears explicitly on the blocked passage from mind to matter, from thinking to its enduring expression in the external world: "Everywhere and without interruption, one was encircled by nothingness, emptiness wholly bereft of space and time" (57). The entwined relationship between space and time, each existing separate from the other, but achieving meaningfulness only when yoked together, is an ancient conundrum. To become perceptible, time requires a mark in the world, as the philosopher Kant so convincingly demonstrated in presenting his view of the human mind. While remaining cyclical, the changing seasons track time by showing its passage in space, in the same way that the before and after of a tsunami or other catastrophe records an event in nature. Humans are models of ingenuity when it comes to fashioning spatial or material signs that hold and measure time; historical consciousness itself - what is most profoundly human - rests squarely on chronologies that punctuate an elusive unfolding, just as calendars, clocks, and other mechanisms of signaling and keeping time. For the imprisoned Dr. B., being subject to the constraints of nothingness meant being deprived of an external bearer of meaning onto which he could latch his thoughts. In the doctor's description of this state of affairs: "One went back and forth, accompanied by thoughts [*die Gedanken*] going back and forth, forth and back, again and again" (57). In a sense, this nothingness refers to a fundamental incongruity between the interior mind and its exteriority; the mind, full of the by-products of its own workings, has nothing to observe, to manipulate, no way to inscribe in the external world its endless ruminations. In the context of this story, applying torture means cutting the mind off from the very possibility of material manifestation, whether it be on the order of expressing thoughts or gaining access to another's thinking through its material existence.

More than a fictional universe, however, this novella presents a full-blown philosophical conception of the external medium without which the mind cannot maintain itself and its power in the world. Certain aspects of this issue are explicit in Zweig's language: "But even thoughts, as intangible [*substanzlos*] as they appear, need a base of support [*Stützpunkt*] without which they begin to turn around themselves and spin off into meaninglessness..." (57). This external anchor, while figurative, refers to a material basis, a focal point which, contrary to thoughts that are insubstantial, without corporeal substance, has physical existence. Meaning itself comes to be on the basis of this interaction, and, ultimately, the interplay between inner and outer, between mind and matter, becomes increasingly linked to forms of lasting material expression, which attest to the process whereby the mind leaves its residue in the world. From the outset, this obsession with material inscription hovers in the background: "The table would hold no book, no newspaper, no paper, and no pencil (...); they had taken away each and every object - my watch, so I wouldn't know the time, my pencil, so I couldn't write, and my knife, so I couldn't open my veins..." (56). This axis of interaction implies necessarily a back-and-forth, as much an expression of the mind's workings, desires, and will, as an engagement with that of other minds. Even the knife, an implement for marking the body to the point of extinguishing its life, is no less a tool of authorship.

In the doctor's telling, the network of references intensifies, introducing new linkages that cast a suggestive light on what is truly at issue. In his situation, he repeats, there was "no distraction, no book, no newspaper, no face of an other [*kein fremdes Gesicht*], no pencil for taking notes, no matches to play with, nothing, nothing, nothing" (61). This distraction is more than simple amusement but provokes a discontinuity in thinking, a turning away [*Ablenkung*] from one's own train of thought, an irruption of otherness, underscored even by the evocation of a stranger's face. In other words, what Zweig points to here concerns the necessity to inscribe thinking in the world, with any of the implements such an act implies, an act simultaneously inseparable from encounters with material traces of others. Refusal of this access to the exterior, inherent in thinking itself, amputates the mind from what it might engender. As the vehicle of this awareness, Dr. B. mused wistfully about how he would have been better off in a concentration camp (61), for him merely a prison of grueling work where, despite the hardship, he imagined being able to see fields and trees, others' faces, things and persons who undergo constant transformation. To say it unequivocally: without matter, the mind is diminished, undergoes violence that this story presents in the guise of torture. In yet another example, the horror of interrogation resulted less from "enhanced" questioning than from the prisoner's observing a "mass of papers" he could not read and watching the transcriptions of information he could not know: "...while you answered, strange [*fremde*] and hostile fingers flipped through papers whose contents you didn't know, and strange and hostile fingers wrote something in the minutes, and you didn't know what they wrote" (59). Or, "I stared, hypnotized, at the pen running across the paper as the minutes were taken, as if I were running after my own words" (63-4). The chase is futile when the inscription of thought is denied.

In the economy of this fictional account, presenting a world of its own, preoccupation with the matter of thought sets the stage for the event that will bring together the chess game, contemporary history, and the broader philosophical question that in the end has little to do with Zweig's novella. During his captivity, Dr. B. happens upon a book, which he quickly appropriates or, rather, "steals." This book - the chess manual I mentioned above - plays a major role in Zweig's story, almost becoming a character in its own right; the doctor's initial encounter, however, is recounted with surgical exactitude:

> [A] book! My knees began to shake: a BOOK! For four months I hadn't held a book in my hands, and already the mere representation [*Vorstellung*] of a book, in which I [*man*] could see strung together words, lines, pages, and leaves, of a book in which I could read, follow other, new, strange, distracting [*ablenkende*] thoughts, keeping them in my head [*sich ins Hirn nehmen könnte*]... (67)

Ultimately, the book - as a concept, an idealized object - furnishes yet another paradigm for matter that records the mind in intending to transmit the fruits of its reflection and leave a legacy for posterity. This passage emphasizes the matter of the book that permits a conceptual understanding of the question at hand, even before it has been touched, stolen, and read. In sum, the book acts here as an exemplary figure that embodies thought as it reflects on its own necessity. Yet the matter that this idea entails cannot be reduced to some modern-day understanding of literary dialogue, criticism, or interpretation. The human is baggage, material baggage, which is the amalgam of intangible thoughts, potential and realized, and their continuing effacement and expression. The human world transcends its present moment only by virtue of the material deposited in it. Without matter, there is no history, just as there is no testimony to the passage of time. This describes human consciousness itself, that of history as well as that of the individual.

The thought experiment conveyed in this narrative makes its most striking universal claim at the story's climax that takes place at the very end. In playing the final match against the grand champion Czentovic, the doctor lost his moorings and began to descend once again into a state of madness; the narrator brought him back to himself by running his finger over the scar while pronouncing only the English word "Remember" (109). As much as any text, the scar is a material mark that proves to be a bearer of history and memory.

Works Cited

Goodwin, Matthew D. "The Brazilian Exile of Vilém Flusser and Stefan Zweig." *Flusser Studies* 07 (Nov. 2008).
Jaccard, Roland. "Introduction" to Stefan Zweig, *Montaigne*, tr. Jean-Jacques Lafaye and François Brugier. Paris: PUF, 2010.
Zweig, Stefan. *Schachnovelle*. Berlin: Fischer, 2008. All translations from this text are mine.

III: RACE AND GENDER IN LITERATURE AND FILM

THE TRIALS OF MOTHERHOOD IN LAUDOMIA BONANNI'S "IL FOSSO"

Joanne Frallicciardi Lyon

The collection of short stories entitled *Il fosso*, published in 1949 by Bompiani, was the first publication of Laudomia Bonanni's mature writing period.[1] The opening story with the same title received the Strega Prize, "Amici della domenica," an award given to an unpublished author. The entire collection was later awarded the Bagutta prize. The setting is the wartime Abruzzi region where Bonanni worked and lived. Her experience as a teacher and later as a judge provided her with the raw material to write. Bonanni recorded the misery and abject poverty of the poorest inhabitants of the region with a sharp, realistic style.

The first story of the collection, "Il fosso," is told from the point of view of the protagonist, who is the biological mother of two children who are also characters in the story. The mother-child relationship is seen not from the daughter's or son's perspective, but from that of the mother. Upon close examination of the text, many feminist themes become apparent, such as the female body, birth control, female sexuality, women as property, women and work, financial affairs, mothering, and the mother-son bond. We will see, in this story, that women become the main protagonists in what is the patriarchal drama of Bonanni's stories.

The story chronicles the life of a young girl, a foundling, who resides in a local convent. The nuns name the child Colomba ("Dove") in honor of the Holy Spirit. The name also invokes an image of purity and whiteness, which sharply contrasts with Colomba's dark complexion. In the opening scene, Colomba is on her way to the Falalani home to work in their tavern. The slight woman, who is twenty years old, seems much younger. The brief physical description is significant in that, later, this wisp of a woman exemplifies a mother with unreserved strength and devotion to her family in the

---

[1] Bonanni's writing career began in 1925 with the publication of *Storie tragiche della montagna*. Between 1925 and 1949 she published a number of children's books, and her first association with Bompiani was in 1939 with the publication of *Men*.

face of adversity. Colomba's magnificent spirit contradicts her delicate figure.

She is soon accepted by all who meet her and is treated with the greatest courtesy. Colombina, as she comes to be known, was never thought to be a candidate for marriage. One can image Signora Falalani's surprise when one day a poor young farmer comes asking for Colomba's hand. Irritated by the request, Signora Falalani sends him to the convent for permission to marry, convinced that it would never be granted. Although intimidated, Titta is nevertheless determined. So one day, at dawn, they marry. At the local tavern, they are toasted: "Figli maschi, figli maschi!"

The ideal patriarchal wish is a family of many sons. Adrienne Rich in her landmark study of motherhood, *Of Woman Born*, tells us that in patriarchy, the mother exists for one reason: "to bear and nourish the son" (188). It is upon the son that all hopes and desires for the future are heaped. The son guarantees the continuation of the bloodline and the family name and thus perpetuates the male desire for immortality (Rich 99). Yet, as we move through the story, we learn that of the two—Colomba and her husband Titta—she is the strongest, suggesting that Bonanni is undermining current beliefs. She depicts mothers as women of strength yet acknowledges society's preference for the male child. Often the daughters are presented as weak and are despised by their mothers for this presumed weakness. These instances indicate Bonanni's keen awareness of a society that places the male in a position of power over the female and of the female's inability to break free of this hold. Although Bonanni denied any association with feminism, her focus on women and in particular mothers strongly suggests that she had observed their personal drama.[2] The patriarchal wish for many sons highlights the prevailing conviction that men will fare better in society and that the male is the empowered individual, thus rendering the female voiceless and powerless. Nevertheless, the men in Bonanni's world are not the privileged sex, as they do not have inner fortitude and are emotionally needy. In fact, their weakness and ineptitude are constantly stressed. Without question, the women are the focus of her stories.

After the toast, the newlyweds leave with Titta's mule. He walks in front of Colomba, who trails behind in her place of submission,

---

[2] Of her feminism, Fiorani writes: "Lei stessa non si riteneva una femminista nell'accezione comune" (50).

until they reach their home, an underground, one-room structure with only one window and a small fireplace.[3] As night falls, Colomba goes to the window and is followed by Titta. He clumsily embraces her, almost imprisoning her with the weight of his body. There the marriage is unceremoniously consummated. Titta claims what is rightfully his—his wife's virginal body. Colomba is quickly impregnated and loses her child one day while working the fields. Adrienne Rich notes that, "historically, woman have borne and raised children while doing their share of necessary productive labor, as a matter of course" (44). Like generations of mothers before them, Colomba never considered any option open to her other than bearing and nurturing children and working simultaneously for survival.

The miscarriage does not surprise the women of the community. Colomba's small body does not seem fit for field labor, much less for childbearing. Yet, soon Colomba finds herself pregnant again, and as her second pregnancy progresses she must stop working the fields to avoid another miscarriage. Her survival skills are put to the test as she discovers alternate ways to earn money. These skills are a sign of her cleverness. One day she gives birth to a child, a daughter, alone. But the town women soon become aware of this and are there to help and give support. The theme of female bonding in times of need is introduced here and maintains a constant presence throughout Bonanni's works. The women share common experiences, observe everything, give advice, pass judgment, and offer assistance. They represent the female voice in a patriarchal society that has often silenced women's voices. "Le donne," like the war, are ever present not only in these stories but throughout many of Bonanni's texts. The women are the collective voice that documents the events and makes comments as the action proceeds.[4] They are the voice of wisdom, a wisdom that represents centuries of experience handed down

---

[3] In a recent study entitled "Laudomia Bonanni, *Il fosso* e *Palma*: il tragico della vita," Giorgio Bàrberi Squarotti describes this space: "È il buco scatologico del mondo, dove anche le piante sono deformi e confuse, ma è vero che il sambuco brutto e scerpato a primavera fa sbocciare i suoi fiori candidi, a dimostrazione che la vita combatte e vince contro l'inverno, la violenza della ragazzaglia, l'arsura dell'estate" (261).

[4] It is interesting to note the use of this same device in the literary movement known as verismo. (See Verga's *I malavoglia*.) Bonanni, however, selects women's voices as the observers and commentators.

by word of mouth. In a sense they are the "foremothers" of this society. Nothing escapes their notice, including the meager living conditions of Titta and Colomba. Indeed, the couple was so poor and
miserable that they did not even have cloths or rags to clean the
blood from the delivery or to wrap the child in. Unable to control her reproductive capacities, Colomba has
fourteen pregnancies, but only one daughter and one son survive. All
the while, she continues to work wherever she can, in the fields, in
the tavern, or in the homes of the wealthy. Motherhood as an institution obliges Colomba to care for her children, keep up their humble
home, prepare meals, and provide clothing, all while also working
outside the home. In Colomba's Italy, the assumption was that the
mother would bear children and also work. Furthermore, she does
not have any control whatsoever over her reproductive capacities. In
a period of twenty years, Colomba is always seen either pregnant or
carrying an infant bundled up to her. After the two surviving children, she had a child yearly—all of whom died. Numerous pregnancies were not unusual. In fact, Titta's parents had ten children with
only one surviving. But Titta and Colomba resign themselves to their
destiny. At work here are the social and economic constructs that
governed women's bodies and the survival of their offspring. In this
backward and mostly illiterate society, the inability to control the
number of pregnancies and the lack of proper nutrition led not only
to numerous pregnancies, but also to a high mortality rate. The notion that the female body was destined to reproduce at any cost was
confirmed in both cultural and religious terms.

One day, while walking and carrying one of her infants bundled
to her chest, Colomba encounters the town priest. Her own desperate situation prompts her to ask him if it isn't a sin to have so many
children. Despite her ignorance and her lack of education, Colomba
instinctively understands that bringing forth more children into their
world of abject poverty and misery, and to an existence of suffering
and dying, is inherently and morally wrong. The priest, normally a
gruff and stern type, gently reproaches her. He seems to understand
her predicament but is unable to assist her. To even consider any
form of birth control in Mussolini's Italy, except perhaps abstinence,
would have been unthinkable. The fascist ideology promoted motherhood as the highest and most honorable participation in the service
of the Italian nation, which can be interpreted as an extreme form of
nationalism and the silencing of the female voice. In 1932, Mussolini

proclaimed that the women must obey and expressed his opposition to any type of feminism (Pickering-Iazzi 78).

Fascist Italy was a dire and oppressive place to live for all Italians but in particular for women. Violence and aggression toward any form of dissent was condoned. Journalists were heavily restricted and censored. Of particular interest is Mussolini's alliance with the Catholic Church. Well aware of the need to have the support of the Church, Mussolini made a concentrated effort to align himself with the pope. Most notable was the Church's cooperation with Mussolini's restrictions concerning women. Mussolini urged families to produce more children. His objective was to encourage an increase in the birth rate and thus allow Italy to compete as a world power with other nations, with a goal to increase the population of Italy from 40 million to 60 million within a twenty-five-year period (Mack-Smith 160). Interestingly enough, the birth rates did not rise, but actually fell. Mussolini's policy restricted the number of women in the workforce, taxed anyone whose celibacy was not justified, and taxed childless marriages. Businesses discriminated by giving hiring preferences to men with families. Divorce was out of the question, as was birth control. Nevertheless, the abortion rate remained as high as 30%. Restrictions were placed on women's dress code and on dancing. Both Mussolini and the Vatican were opposed to women participating in any so-called "masculine sports" (160–61). Without question, Mussolini and fascist ideology did much to perpetuate patriarchal attitudes and practices in Italy while at the same time crushing feminism as a movement.[5]

Colomba struggles to survive in this hostile, anti-feminist, and oppressive environment. She is not able to care for her children, as her days are consumed with work. As long as her children are nursing, she can keep them with her, but once they are weaned, she is forced to leave them on their own in the garden. When her children are older, Colomba enrolls them in school. But the children are incapable of formulating any abstract ideas or of sitting still to listen to their lessons. Not surprisingly, the school experience is a source of agitation for Colomba. The children eventually follow pre-selected

---

[5] Victoria De Grazia states: ". . . fascists condemned all the social practices customarily connected with the emancipation of women—from the vote and female participation in the labor force to family planning. They also sought to extirpate the very attitudes and behaviors of individual self-interest that underlay women's demands for equality and autonomy" (2).

paths according to their gender: Onorina stays home and learns to sew, and Innocenzo finds creative ways to earn money. When Onorina becomes ill with a fever, the doctor is called. But upon seeing Colomba pregnant yet another time, the doctor is more concerned for her health than for the child. He places the blame for Colomba's many pregnancies on her husband and advises him to consider abstinence. A bewildered Titta wonders if he is truly responsible. Perhaps Bonanni uses this episode to point a finger at the Italian society's barring couples from using any form of birth control. Indeed, in fascist Italy, Mussolini urged women to have large families with little or no regard for their health. Titta, thinking he is to blame, turns pale with fear. In his ignorance he assumes that he has the right to be with his wife and is not aware that in satisfying his sexual needs he is at the same time compromising his wife's health. The sudden realization upon hearing his doctor's comment and understanding its implications compel Titta to face a reality for which he was not prepared. This is a life-changing moment for him and, not knowing how to proceed, he begins to spend less and less time at home and takes to drinking. Bonanni here clearly faults a society that had refused to consider the rights of women. In her encompassing view, both males and females are victims.

However, Colomba's thoughts, as well as Titta's, are focused on their daughter. As they are unable to provide the necessary medical care for her, Onorina has been entrusted to a young nun. Giving her up is a very traumatic experience, and at this time Colomba delivers a stillborn child. Quite clearly the mother and father were unable to stop the process and prevent further pregnancies. They were trapped in a system that was not capable of assisting them in any kind of planned parenthood. Even the concept was a taboo topic, and any form of birth control was not to be a reality until decades later. Women were powerless to limit the number of children they bore. In her chapter entitled "The 'Sacred Calling,'" Rich discusses the notion of motherhood and woman's work in the home: "The real, depleting burdens of motherhood were physical: the toll of continual pregnancies, the drain of constant childbearing and nursing" (48). Women like Colomba were victims of a patriarchal institution that controlled every aspect of their reproductive capacities. Years of hard physical labor, numerous pregnancies, lack of proper nutrition, and the psychological toll of sending her daughter away result in a sharp decline in Colomba's health.

Then one day, Colomba makes a most important discovery: "il Governo" (Bonanni 36). She learns to take advantage of the government assistance programs, knocking on doors and waiting for hours in luxurious waiting rooms. She is successful in receiving full compensation from the government for her daughter's entire medical bill. She also receives benefits for all of her fourteen children; the fact that only two were living is inconsequential. She quickly perceives that her fourteen pregnancies make quite an impression on the fascist government as, after all, Mussolini himself had urged women to bear more children. Colomba is well informed, knowing that her only living son cannot be called into service. And for this only living son she will milk "il Governo" now that she has discovered it (36–37). The townsfolk and the men in the city hall marvel at her survival skills.

The war figures prominently in Bonanni's early works. Here, too, it heaps more misery upon the townsfolk, but not on Colomba. Assured that they cannot take her son, and now with only two mouths to feed (Onorina no longer lives with them, and Titta has been committed to a mental institution), Colomba is managing much better than most. In her urge to survive, Colomba shows not only strength of character but also a certain wit and intelligence. She has profited from government subsidy programs and emerges unscathed from the wartime misery.

In her final years, Colomba receives news of her daughter's death.[6] Shocked by the tragedy, she falls into a somewhat catatonic state. Thinking his mother is dying, Innocenzo calls for help. But the doctor finds Colomba still breathing. She moans as the doctor probes her depleted, worn-out body. It is a moan that is filled with all the sadness and misery of her life (47). At the end of the story, the metaphor of the ditch —"il fosso"—becomes apparent. Colomba and her family are buried deeply in the misery of this ditch that represents the family's dire poverty. Yet, despite all the suffering, life must continue; Innocenzo finds work doing manual labor, and Colomba returns to preparing Innocenzo's meals. The narrator notes that Colomba's movements, lacking strength and agility, resemble

---

[6] In his article, Giorgio Bàrbieri Squarotti argues that this scene represents one of Bonanni's high points as writer and observer of life: "L'epicedio di Onorina morta . . . è una delle più alte pagine del romanzo, e, forse, di tutti gli altri romanzi della Bonanni, per l'intensità e la chiarezza della consapevolezza della tragicità assoluta che è la vita" (262).

that of a broken serpent. The final image is that of a woman, a dedicated mother, consumed physically and mentally, whose will to survive remains unbroken.

Works Cited

Bonanni, Laudomia. *Il fosso*. Milano: Mondadori, 1949.

De Grazia, Victoria. *How Fascism Ruled Women: Italy, 1922–1945*. Berkeley: U of California P, 1992.

Fiorani, Alfredo. *Laudomia Bonanni: Il solipsismo di genere femminile*. Chieti: Edizioni Noubs, 2007.

Mack Smith, Denis. *Mussolini*. New York: Vintage Books, 1982.

Pickering-Iazzi, Robin Wynette. *Mothers of Invention: Women, Italian Fascism, and Culture*. Minneapolis: U of Minnesota P, 1995.

Rich, Adrienne Cecile. *Of Women Born: Motherhood as Experience and Institution*. 10th anniversary ed. New York: Norton, 1986.

Squarotti, Giorgio Bárberi. "Laudomia Bonanni, Il fosso e Palma: Il tragico della vita." *Campi immaginabili: Rivista Semestrale della Cultura* 40–41 (2009): 254–76.

ALL THE SINGLE LADIES:
'WORKING GIRLS' IN WEIMAR GERMANY

Aneka Meier

During the Weimar years, heated debates raged around the so-called New Woman, who had allegedly entered both "public space and popular imagination as a mass phenomenon" after World War I. Even though she "had existed as a Bohemian or professional rarity and literary convention" (Grossman, "Girlkultur" 65) before the war—early Expressionist writer Else Lasker-Schüler and the free-spirited intellectual Lou Andreas-Salomé are prominent examples—, this independent woman did not gain visibility until later. The New Woman emerged as a peculiar necessity during the war when she initially had to take over men's jobs and became a subject of intense fascination in the early 1920s when the economic crisis forced many women to take on gainful employment.

The independent single woman in German and American culture alike was widely considered immoral and decadent. Ashley Nelson, who compares Carrie Bradshaw from the television series *Sex and the City* with Sister Carrie from Theodore Dreiser's 1900 novel of the same name, points out that a "woman's decision to support herself has also often led to ruinous innuendoes about her sexuality": "Frequently cast as overly sexual, single women have long been told their sexuality would cost them—if not their lives, then at least a good man. Doubleday, after all, nearly refused to publish 'Sister Carrie' because Dreiser failed to place any moral judgment on Carrie's romping lifestyle. If only she had died from syphilis, they argued" (Nelson 85). *Sister Carrie* transgressed all contemporary morality:

> …Carrie is immoral, living with two men out of wedlock… but even worse, she never pays the wages of sin. Indeed she prospers! What a terrible example to young American womanhood, whom the censorship laws were designed to protect. (Lingeman xvii)

Walter Ruttmann's 1927 film *Berlin. Die Sinfonie der Großstadt* presents multiple New Women on the streets, highlighting the many facets of women's new presence in the metropolis. Despite women's increased visibility in the city, women who appeared alone in public were immediately understood as sexually available. Atina Grossmann explains why progressive women were often misinterpreted as prostitutes: The New Woman "bobbed her hair, smoked in public, shaved her legs, used makeup; indeed, presented herself in such a manner that it sometimes became difficult to distinguish the 'honest women' from the 'whores'" (Grossman, "Desire" 156). Sabine Hake points out that "until the war, only prostitutes and demimondaines wore makeup during the day" (Hake 189). Red lipstick in particular symbolized *Anrüchigkeit*, indecency. A caricature by Rudolf Kriesch, which is included in Kracauer's essay "Mädchen im Beruf" in the magazine *Querschnitt* from April 1932 illustrates this public perception. It shows two young women, presumably sisters, both dressed up and ready to go out, while their parents sit at the table, reading the newspaper. When their father, in clear disapproval of their look, asks them, "Wohin so spät? Ihr treibt es ja wie die Kokotten!," they respond: "Nanu, sollen wir vielleicht stenographieren?" The traditional female cliché in its Madonna/Whore polarity no longer applies to Weimar girls and their self-representation in the city street. In his analysis of the street scenes in Ruttmann's film, Siegfried Kracauer comes to the following conclusion: "The many prostitutes among the passers-by also indicate that society has lost its balance" (Kracauer 186). Pivotal to his argument is one particular street scene which he misreads and which has been widely misinterpreted by other scholars. Janet Ward Lungstrum, for instance, notes that the "pickup of a male passer-by by a female prostitute literally occurs through the right angle of a corner store's two windows" (Ward Lungstrum 150). Taking a closer look at this particular sequence, it becomes apparent that the viewer deals with at least four different women here, and the couple walking by in the subsequent shot, seen by Kracauer as implying successful solicitation, is, in fact, a completely different man and woman. Even today, many of the discussions surrounding modern womanhood and stigmas against female singles remain unchanged, as a quote from the popular 2011 movie *Bridesmaids* shows: "You can't go to the wedding alone. If you go alone, people might think you're a prostitute."

A fine line between white-collar work and prostitution was rapidly established in Weimar popular culture. As a means of securing temporary pleasure and economic stability and of achieving social advancement, the Weimar working woman employs her body as commodity. In exchange for sensual, or in many cases downright

sexual favors, the female characters in many novels and movies during that time are given luxury items, clothes, housing, and food. Often engaging in a lucrative love affair with their boss, they make use
of their 'sex appeal' in order to either secure or improve their position. As women are reduced—or reduce themselves—to mere commodities, relationships are solely based on monetary exchange.
Commodification plays out on different levels, with prostitution representing its most extreme form.

Fully aware of her sexual exchange value and using her attrac-
tiveness to her advantage, Doris from Irmgard Keun's 1932 novel
The Artificial Silk Girl employs her body as an instrument for obtain-
ing a better life, allowing herself to be kept by men. According to her
motto "Hübsche Mädchen sind ein Geschäft" (111), she chooses a
male-sponsored life in order to make her dream of upward mobility a
reality and to achieve the status of *Glanz,* "the shimmering image of a
beautiful woman propagated in late Weimar culture by its advertising
and consumer culture, its fashion industry, as well as the star system
of both the German film industry and of Hollywood" (McCormick
133). She starts out as a 'gold digger,' engaging in relationships with
men who can provide her with the glamorous lifestyle she desires.
She insists on material compensation for her company and sexual
favors:

> Sie zieht aus den Gegebenheiten der unverhohlen
> kapitalistischen Gesellschaft (wie der Roman sie zeigt) ihre
> eigenen Schlüsse: Selbstbewußtsein wird durch Kaufkraft
> erreicht, die materiellen Güter, 'Fetische des Fortschritts',
> wiegen Bildungsdefizite auf, Schönheit und Jugend müssen
> als, Tauschwert' herhalten, solange das Ziel nicht erreicht ist.
> Ihr hektisches Agieren, ihr Bemühen um kaltschnäuzige
> Sachlichkeit, ihr freizügiges erotisches Verhalten, ihr
> Bemühen, sich elegant und anziehend auszustaffieren,
> stehen ganz im Dienst dieses Aufstiegswunsches. (Rosen-
> stein 180-181)

In the beginning, the systematical strategies Doris employs in
order to accumulate material goods or simply have a good time are
still modest. She manipulates men into replacing her broken watch
with a new one or buying a new outfit for her. After Doris becomes
unemployed, because she refuses to have an affair with her boss, she
nevertheless immediately tries to turn to another man for help:
"Aber jetzt sitze ich noch mit 80 Mark und ohne neue Existenz und

frage mich nur, wo ist nun ein Mann für meine Notlage" (28). She realizes that there is no job she could have that would grant her the lifestyle and material abundance she dreams of and that the only way of achieving the status of *Glanz* is to find a man who is able to provide her with the public display of wealth and material comfort that she strives for. Disillusioned by the prospect of getting ahead economically through her own labor, and the realization that social recognition and economic security can only be achieved through relationships with men, she 'sells' herself.[1] In order to attract such men, she frequents many cafés, bars and nightclubs. The men expect sexual favors in return, while Doris is completely aware of this 'exchange of commodities':

> [Er] bot mir eine Wohnung und Geld—mir kam die Gelegenheit zu einem Glanz, und es ist leicht mit Alten, wenn man jung ist—sie tun, als könnte man was dafür, und als hätte man es geleistet. Und ich wollte, ich wollte. Er hatte eine Kegelkugelstimme, die mich kalt macht, aber ich wollte—er hatte so verschleimtes Gelüge in den Augen, aber ich wollte—ich dachte, die Zähne zusammenbeißen und an machtvolle Hermeline denken, dann geht es. (86)

When Doris is faced by the prospect of becoming a prostitute later on in the story, the city street is still depicted as place of display, commodity circulation, and business transactions, but now, because of the economic situation, it is dominated by 'the oldest trade in the world':

> Und gestern war ich mit einem Mann, was mich ansprach und für was hielt, was ich doch nicht bin. Ich bin es doch noch nicht. Aber überall stehen Huren—am Alex so viele, so viele—auf dem Kurfürstendamm und Joachimsthaler und am Friedrichsbahnhof und überall. Und sehn gar nicht immer aus wie welche, sie machen so einen unentschlossenen Gang—das ist gar nicht immer das Gesicht, was eine Hure so ausmacht—ich sehe in meinen Spiegel—das ist eine Art von Gehen, wie wenn einem das Herz eingeschlafen ist. (144)

Her selective portrayal of the street consequently consists of nothing but prostitutes on street corners. As prostitution is now

---

[1] See Von Ankum, "Material Girls" 162-163 and Smail 74-75.

omnipresent, all glamour is gone. Whenever she stops in the street, she is assumed to be a prostitute: "Und dann sprach mich einer an, das war so ein Besserer, ich sagte: 'Ich bin nicht *mein Kind* für Sie, ich bin eine Dame'" (145). She cannot stop and lean against the corner of a building, because by doing so she would be implying that she, like everything else on display, can be bought. And yet Doris gradually starts to identify herself unwittingly with the streetwalkers by the way she walks: "Immer ging ich weiter, die Huren stehen an den Ecken und machen ihren Sport, und in mir war eine Maschinenart, die genau ihr Gehen und Stehenbleiben machte" (145). Artificial silk girl Doris is familiar with the milieu of the *halbseidenen Mädchen*[2] through the prostitute Hulla. As the story progresses, the distance that formerly separated her life from Hulla's becomes increasingly smaller. Later, Doris expresses sympathy for Hulla who had jumped out of a window out of fear of her pimp Rannowsky:

> Die Hulla war eine Hure, vielleicht hat solche kein Grab, und man macht den Menschen das Leben auf der Erde manchmal wohl zu schwer und darum ist es ganz albern für sie zu beten, wenn sie dann glücklich tot ist. Und wenn es keine Männer gibt, die bezahlen, dann gibt es doch auch keine Hullas—kein Mann darf Schlechtes über die Hulla sagen. Ich wünsche ihr wirklich einen Himmel, in dem das Gute in ihren Augen Verwendung findet. Und wenn sie ein Engel ist, dann soll sie Flügel haben ohne Leukoplast geklebt. (136)

Doris comes to realize that Hulla's fate is the possible prefiguring of her own.

At the end of her journey, Doris is only steps away from being reduced to the cheapest commodity, the streetwalker, facing an uncertain future. Destitute and marginalized from society, her only options of survival are either living with her friend Karl in a *Laubenkolonie* outside of Berlin or joining the multitude of prostitutes she notices everywhere in the city. Disillusioned, she realizes that her search for glamour is over (—which, in fact, may not be so important after all): "Ich bin ja immer das Mädchen vom Wartesaal" (210) and "Auf den Glanz kommt es nämlich vielleicht gar nicht so furchtbar an" (219). She has come to learn a hard lesson and also

---

[2] The German term *halbseidenes Mädchen* generally refers to a 'dubious woman,' in particular a prostitute.

implicitly questions the notion of emancipation for all women at this time. In her reading of Keun's novel in the discourse of prostitution, Katharina von Ankum argues that Doris' "experience of the city is that of the New Woman of the 1920s—doomed to failure in the metropolis in spite of her newly won professional and sexual freedoms—because the patriarchal economic structures have remained intact" (Von Ankum, "Gendered Urban Spaces" 169).

Erna Halbe, the 19-year-old protagonist in Rudolf Braune's *Das Mädchen an der Orga Privat* (1930), observes her female colleagues' dating games. In their approach less aggressive and calculating than Doris, the *Büromädels* all rely on their boyfriends to purchase them clothes, pay for a movie visit, a weekend outing, and other leisure activities. Economic and social factors play a predominant role and they have relationships with the opposite sex to supplement their meager salary or to assist them financially once they become unemployed: "Ehe ich krepiere, suche ich mir doch einen Freund" (53). Another typist states: "Gott, wenn ihr kein Geld habt, müßt ihr euch eben einen Kavalier nehmen. Tut doch nicht so" (61). Hereby, most girls differentiate between the man that supports them financially and the one they truly love. Erna, a morally upright working-class girl from the provinces, has just arrived in the city and is stunned by her new colleagues' behavior. As she neither aspires to stardom nor tries to immediately find a husband, she cannot understand why some of the other office girls engage in affairs with the managers Siodmak and Lortzing. One of the typists enlightens her: "Liebe Erna, du bist ein nettes Mädel, aber überlege dir bitte mal, wie du mit hundertzwanzig Mark, oder wieviel du ausgezahlt bekommst, in Berlin leben willst" (64). This remark corresponds with Kracauer's diagnosis: "Natürlich wissen sie, daß sie bei dem geringen Einkommen einen Freund haben müßten, wenn sie keine Angehörigen besäßen" (Kracauer, "Die Angestellten" 69). Referring to desires like going to the movies, attending concerts, or traveling, Kracauer notes in his essay "Mädchen im Beruf" (1932) accordingly: "Wenn die Mädchen solche luxuriöse Bedürfnisse haben, deren Befriedigung in Wahrheit kein Luxus ist, sind sie einfach darauf angewiesen, freigehalten zu werden. Der Freund ist eine erotische und materielle Notwendigkeit zugleich" (Kracauer, "Mädchen" 242).

This is also true for another Weimar woman, the attractive hotel stenographer Flämmchen, who is the star of Vicki Baum's 1929 bestseller *Menschen im Hotel*, a novel treating issues such as vulnerable masculinity and unsettled female sexuality. The grand hotel, a major player in the novel itself, can be viewed as microcosm of modernity and its upheavals. Baum highlights sexuality, prostitution, and women's role in Weimar society as personified in Flämmchen, who appears as the incarnation of the New Woman. She relies on men to reward her company and sexual favors with temporary financial stability and short-lived pleasures. In addition to her typing job, Flämmchen also works as an escort for wealthy businessmen (what we would refer to today as a 'call-girl'). Absolutely unsentimental, pragmatic, and ambitious, she has neither illusions about life and love nor expects a 'knight in shining armor' to save her, and "she has no reservations about selling herself to earn enough to get by" (King 187). As an inspiration to male fantasies and an erotic spectacle, she is both an object of male desire and a threat to male sexuality: "Her image is often rendered in terms of a cat or a (race) horse, and this alignment with brute creation in turn characterizes her as a creature close to nature with the unfettered libido so threatening to patriarchal law and order" (Petersen 83). Through her job, Flämmchen meets Generaldirektor Preysing, a provincial industrialist, who asks her to be his paid companion, inviting her to spend several nights with him at the hotel, and then accompany him to England on his next business trip. Engaging her 'sex appeal' in order to land a job, she employs her body as her most valuable asset in exchange for money and clothing: "Sie kannte ihren Preis. Zwanzig Mark für eine Aktaufnahme. Hundertvierzig Mark für einen Monat Büroarbeit. Fünfzehn Pfennig für eine Seite Schreibarbeit mit Durchschlag. Ein Pelzmäntelchen zu zweihundertvierzig Mark für eine Woche Hingabe" (297). Vibeke Petersen points out that "both Flämmchen and Doris rely on their youth and sexual desirability to men for their material survival which only confirms that it is male rather than female privilege that is the final arbiter of the discourse of female independence" (Petersen 38).

It has become increasingly clear that the consensus view is that the city is dominated by the commodity character of relationships. In her study *Joyless Streets. Women and Melodramatic Representation in Weimar*, one of the most important works on Weimar popular culture and women, Patrice Petro focuses on the juxtaposing of women and cities which became evident in the general discourse of modernity, but for her Berlin "served as the decisive metaphor for modernity. Modernity," she continues, "in turn was almost always represented as a woman" (Petro 40). We then note how Walter Benjamin's ambivalence toward mass cultural distraction and his fear of and fascination with mass culture is often projected onto the figure of woman, and in particular that of the prostitute (Petro 60). The inscription of prostitution in Weimar Berlin also figures prominently in Weimar poetry and art, especially in urban images by Georg Grosz and Otto Dix, as well as in the portrayal of the city in poems by Erich Kästner and Walter Mehring. In many works of the Weimar period, the metropolis was portrayed as Sodom und Gomorrha or the *Hure Babylon* (Whore Babylon), a topos that had already gained significance before World War I, specifically in early Expressionist poetry. It comes out clearly in art, especially in Ernst Ludwig Kirchner's paintings, as well as in Bertolt Brecht's portrayal of women as whores, particularly in his play *Die Dreigroschenoper*, which premiered in Berlin in 1928. In Alfred Döblin's novel *Berlin Alexanderplatz* (1929) the apocalyptic image, taken from the book of *Revelations* (17, 18), is the symbol of evil, a force that will lead to the city's inevitable destruction. The allegory of the Whore Babylon embodies the seductive potential of Berlin as metropolis, with all its temptations, born of its system of capitalism.

Works Cited

Ankum, Katharina von. "Gendered Urban Spaces in Irmgard Keun's 'Das kunstseidene Mädchen.'" *Women in the Metropolis: Gender and Modernity in Weimar Culture.* Ed. Katharina von Ankum. Berkeley, Los Angeles, London: University of California Press, 1997. 162-184.

---. "Material Girls: Consumer Culture and the 'New Woman' in Anita Loos' 'Gentlemen Prefer Blondes' and Irmgard Keun's 'Das kunstseidene Mädchen.'" *Colloquia Germanica* 27. 2 (1994): 159-172.

Baum, Vicki. *Menschen im Hotel.* Köln: Kiepenheuer & Witsch, 2002.

Braune, Rudolf. *Das Mädchen an der Orga Privat.* Frankfurt am Main: Glotzi, 2002.

Dreiser, Theodore. *Sister Carrie.* New York: Signet, 2000.

Grossmann, Atina. "'Girlkultur' or Thoroughly Rationalized Female: A New Woman in Weimar Germany?." *Women in Culture and Politics: A Century of Change*, Ed. Judith Friedlander, Blanche Wiesen Cook, Alice Kessler-Harris, and Caroll Smith-Rosenberg. Bloomington: Indiana University Press, 1986. 62-80.

---. "The New Woman and the Rationalization of Sexuality in Weimar Germany." *Powers of Desire: The Politics of Sexuality*. Ed. Ann Snitow, Christine Stansell, and Sharon Thompson. New York: Monthly Review Press, 1983. 153-171.

Hake, Sabine. "In the Mirror of Fashion." *Women in the Metropolis: Gender and Modernity in Weimar Culture*. Ed. Katharina von Ankum. Berkeley, Los Angeles, London: University of California Press, 1997. 185-201.

Keun, Irmgard. *Das kunstseidene Mädchen*. 3rd ed. München: List, 2002.

King, Lynda J. "Grand Hotel: The Sexual Politics of a Popular Culture Classic." *Women in German Yearbook* 16 (2000): 185-2000.

Kracauer, Siegfried. *Die Angestellten: Aus dem neuesten Deutschland*. Frankfurt am Main: Suhrkamp, 1971.

---. From Caligari to Hitler: A Psychological History of the German Film. Princeton: Princeton University Press, 1947.

---. "Mädchen im Beruf." *Querschnitt* 12.4 (1932): 238-243.

Lingeman, Richard. Introduction, *Sister Carrie*, by Theodore Dreiser. New York: Signet, 2000.

McCormick, Richard W. Gender and Sexuality in Weimar Modernity: Film, Literature, and 'New Objectivity.'" New York: palgrave, 2001.

Meier, Aneka. Working Girls: Fictional Representation of Female Office Workers in Weimar Germany. Diss. University of Florida, 2008.

Nelson, Ashley. "Sister Carrie meets Carrie Bradshaw: Exploring Progress, Politics and the Single Woman in 'Sex and the City' and beyond," *Reading Sex and the City*. Ed. Kim Akass and Janet McCabe. London; New York: I.B. Tauris, 2004.

Petersen, Vibeke Rützou. Women and Modernity in Weimar Germany: Reality and its Representation in Popular Fiction. New York, Oxford: Berghahn Books, 2001.

Petro, Patrice. *Joyless Streets: Women and Melodramatic Representation in Weimar Germany*. Princeton, New Jersey: Princeton University Press, 1989.

Rosenstein, Doris. "'Mit der Wirklichkeit auf du und du?': Zu Irmgard Keuns Romanen ‚Gilgi, eine von uns' und ‚Das kunstseidene Mädchen.'" *Neue Sachlichkeit im Roman: Neue Interpretationen zum Roman der Weimarer Republik*. Ed. Sabina Becker and Christoph Weiß. Stuttgart, Weimar: Metzler, 1995. 273-290.

Smail, Deborah. White-collar workers, Mass Culture and Neue Sachlichkeit in Weimar Berlin: A Reading of Hans Fallada's ‚Kleiner Mann – Was Nun?,' Erich Kästner's ‚Fabian' and Irmgard Keun's ‚Das kunstseidene Mädchen.' Bern, Berlin, Frankfurt am Main, New York, Paris, Wien: Lang, 1999.

Ward Lungstrum, Janet. "The Display Window: Designs and Desires of Weimar Consumerism." *New German Critique* 76 (1999): 115-160.

AN UNNATURAL HISTORY OF SPECIES IN THE FICTION OF VERCORS AND LAURENCE GONZALES

Mary Sanders Pollock

As Levi-Strauss has famously proclaimed, animals are "good to think with." Given its historical context, Vercors's *Les Animaux Denaturés* is clearly a work in which species functions as a metaphor for race and ethnicity. However, the novel also lends itself to a more literal reading as a story about the exploitation of non-human animals, and retains a surprising relevance in discourse about the fluid nature of species boundaries—an even more vexed question now than it was in post-Nazi Europe. In the late twentieth and early twenty-first centuries, thinking *about* animals, not merely *with* them, has become a moral imperative, partly because the separation of "us" and "them" is not as much of a sure thing as it used to be and partly because humans have exploited or endangered nearly every other species on the planet.

A participant of the French resistance, Vercors (pseudonym of Jean Marcel Bruller) organized underground publishing activities during the Nazi occupation, but his own writing clearly transcends propaganda. In his best known work, "Le Silence de la Mer," a short novel published in 1941, the protagonist, a German soldier, is beset by francophilia and embarrassment at being quartered with a French family, but he lacks the ethical refinement to understand his own discomfort. Similarly, in *Les Animaux Denatures*, published in Paris in 1952, Vercors' protagonist struggles to understand his own position in unfamiliar ethical territory.

The subsequent history of the novel suggests something about its generic and thematic ambiguity. Within three years, it had been translated into English by the author's wife Rita Barisse and published three more times—in 1953 by Little, Brown as *You Shall Know Them* in 1954 by Macmillan as *Borderline*; and in 1955 by Pocket Books as *The Murder of the Missing Link*. The provocative cover of the Pocket Books edition (a ghostly hand holding a syringe, outlined in red and superimposed on a frightened blonde) suggests both speculative fiction and a murder mystery—and was evidently meant to sell copies in bus terminals and train stations. Finally, in 1970, the book was loosely adapted into a horror film entitled *Skullduggery*, starring Burt Reynolds and Susan Clarke.

The generic ambiguity derives from the novel's premise and an ending which resists closure. *Les Animaux Denatures* reflects the mid twentieth century anxiety about a destructive synthesis of political philosophy, genetics, and eugenics in service of political and military power (Hobsbaum 252-56). Since National Socialist (or colonial capitalist) rhetoric casts certain human beings as animals, Vercors's literary riposte is to take this notion to its logical conclusion: let's imagine, he suggests, how the missing link might really look and behave.

In the novel, a team of scientists realize that their discovery in New Guinea of a new species of ape men will result in the creatures' enslavement by an Australian textile firm, which owns extractive rights to the area. To forestall this outcome, the scientists artificially inseminate several of the females with materials from Douglas Templemore, a journalist with the expedition. (Later, everyone realizes more sperm donors should have been included in the project.) The scientists hope to prove that the *anthropithecus graemius*, or "tropis," as the new species has been informally designated, are human, and thus entitled to human rights. Not only are the tropis themselves at risk: their existence reopens frightening questions about race and rights that have not been put to rest, despite the experience of the Holocaust. "Why is it," asks the Lord Privy Seal at one point

> that we see the Nuremberg Laws, in spite of all the hopes that went into their making, gradually dissolving into shadows, and in those shadows, new crimes prepared? (160)

Although the scientists seem vaguely aware that inseminating the females without their consent already violates the tropis' human rights, this expedient, they hope, will provide an answer which the biologists, anthropologist, and missionary on the team have been unable to answer on taxonomic, cultural, or religious grounds. However, as is often the case when technoscience gets involved, there are unintended consequences.

Back in London, Templemore and his wife Frances care for Derry, the female tropi farthest along in her pregnancy. After her delivery, Templemore carries out the second part of the plan—all the more important because the infant is distinctly ape-like (especially in its feet, which resemble hands): the birth is registered, the baby christened, the baby killed by a lethal injection, a doctor summoned to pronounce the cause of death, and the police called in to take Templemore into custody. By design, the outcome of his murder trial will determine the tropis' species status.

Vercors may have chosen an English setting because, unlike the Napoleonic Code, which would have been more familiar to his French readers, English Common Law places the burden of proof of guilt on the prosecution of a crime: the "tests" for guilt are more stringent and, for first-degree murder, include the requirement that the victim be human. There is no doubt Templemore killed the baby—his own baby. But is it murder? Only if the tropis are human! If he is convicted, he will hang, but the tropis will not be enslaved because they are legally considered human; if he is found not guilty of murder, the tropis will be the property of the textile company, and Templemore's sacrifices will have been in vain.

Not surprisingly, the judge's uncertainty is transmitted to a nervous jury, who cannot decide the case because, it turns out, no satisfactory definition of "the human" exists. The question is tossed over to a Parliamentary commission who, after lengthy wrangling and discoursing, ultimately define "the human" broadly as a "denatured" being: consciously alienated from nature, humans reveal their alienation in various "religious impulses," including charms ("jujus") and cannibalism.

The tropis are odd creatures, and a few of them will do anything for canned ham, including voluntary incarceration at the scientists base camp. (Perhaps this detail is enough to suggest Vercors' subtle humor throughout the text.) Although the "tamed" tropis do not meet the religion test, those who refused to enter the expedition camp do. First, the untamed tropis have been ritually consumed by the expedition porters, Papuan cannibals who eat other humans in order to incorporate their powers. The implication is that it takes one (a "primitive" human) to know one. Second, the untamed tropis smoke their meat briefly, evidently to purify it but not to cook it. When the untamed tropis can manage to get canned ham, they still smoke it. And if some tropis are deemed human, all of them must be considered human.

Even with the definition offered by the Parliamentary commission, which affirms the membership of the tropis in the human race, Douglas goes free because the tropis' humanity was not established before he killed the infant. Furthermore, the tropis will not be enslaved because they are now considered human. In spite of this ostensibly happy ending, Douglas and Frances are not pleased with the verdict because the abstemious definition of the "human" does not advance the discussion of race and rights—a subject which has raised its ugly head at every turn during their ordeal—in the press, in the courts, and in private conversations.

The tropis were for Vercors a metaphor for marginalized peoples in the colonized global south and elsewhere, and the Holocaust a grim reminder that marginalizing and dehumanizing any human outgroup leads to moral collapse. He was not interested in the rights of animals. But sixty years later, the question of the human has become even more complex, and human rights are still violated continually in many parts of the world.

In any case, many contemporary societies across the planet do now consider animal rights seriously. In *The Great Ape Project*, published in 1993, Peter Singer and Paola Cavalieri collected statements by better than thirty internationally recognized figures in psychology, evolutionary biology, philosophy, ethics, and primatology. They are, collectively, somewhat like the assemblages of experts in Vercors' novel. Like Templemore, the editors of this volume wish to expand "the moral community" (311). Specifically, the project aims to assure the great apes' rights to life and individual liberty, and to protect them from torture (4).

Penelope Nussbaum has pointed out that, in rights discourse, "the individual" typically replaces "the species" (B7). However, in arguing for rights for certain species such as bonobos, chimpanzees, gorillas, and orangutans, contributors to *The Great Ape Project* focus on "species as a collectivity, and. . . opt for (otherwise questionable) rigid [species] boundaries" (310). In the conclusion to the book, Cavalieri and Singer argue that framing the issue in this way parallels the legal emancipations of enslaved human persons during the nineteenth and twentieth centuries: general emancipation succeeds better than manumission on a case by case basis.

Les Animaux Denatures belongs to a long tradition of speculative work about the human-animal borderline, and it was a precursor, if not a model, for the Great Ape Project. The number of similar fictions *following* the Great Ape Project is too long to enumerate here, but it includes a pair of science fiction trilogies by David Brin (1980-1998); "Rachel in Love," a science fiction short novel by Patricia Murphy (1987); *Eva*, an adolescent novel by Peter Dickinson (1988); *The Woman and the Ape,* a speculative novel by Peter Høeg (1996); *Wish* (1995) by Peter Goldsworthy; *The Evolution of Bruno Littlemore* by Benjamin Hale (2011); and the second novel under consideration here, *Lucy*, by Laurence Gonzales (2010). All these works feature biological or cybernetic hybrid ape-human characters—all too human, in all but DNA. Together, they present a temptation to read Vercors's work slightly out of context, as a speculative work about the treatment and mistreatment of non-human animals.

The title character of Gonzales's science thriller is a "species of one"—the offspring of a genetically altered bonobo provocatively named Leda and Dr. Stone, a secretive primatologist who has spent most of his professional life studying these apes in Congo (251). Lucy's unique position puts her at special risk. After her father falls victim to civil war, Lucy, genetically his daughter and perhaps his granddaughter as well, is rescued and brought to the United States by another bonobo researcher, Jenny Lowe, who only gradually comes to understand Lucy's origins because Lucy seems (superficially, at least) to be a perfectly normal child. When the secret leaks out, Jenny's small family is besieged by the media, various intelligence agencies, and, most dangerous of all, a secret group of neo-Nazi religious zealots.

Like the team of scientists in Vercors' novel, even though Stone created Lucy with good intentions—to save the bonobos and improve the human race by breeding into it their emotional generosity--his work was ethically horrifying. His lovely daughter lives because of it, but she also suffers. Unlike the tropis, Lucy finds her rights swept away, even after defending her humanity eloquently in a Congressional hearing: "As any legitimate scientist will tell you, a human is a type of ape," she begins. Humans are descended from a long line of archaic great apes.

> I am born of *Homo sapiens* and *Pan paniscus*, two forms of ape. So I, too, am a new type of human. And so I say: I am human, and I am ape. You are, too, as is everyone in this room. (189)

And when Lucy goes on to quote Portia's speech on the quality of mercy (from *The Merchant of Venice*), scarcely a dry eye remains in the chamber.

Although Gonzales's narrator does not say so, insofar as Lucy has a legal status at all, it derives from the "one drop" rule in the pre-Civil War United States, which declared any individual with any African ancestry to be a Negro and a potential slave. And unfortunately, rather than allaying fear and suspicion, Lucy's impressive intellectual gifts—a combination of bonobo perception with human intelli-

gence—create panic and paranoia. No one within the power structure makes the ethical stand required to protect her: Lucy's existence
may be frightening, but it is also potentially useful in military research. So she is kidnapped; imprisoned in the primate laboratory in
Alamagordo; subjected to a series of painful tests by a primate veter-
inarian; and slated to be euthanized when the tests are completed.

Lucy's bonobo strength and reflexes enable her to escape, but
nothing can save her from cold exploitation or the religious crazies
except living entirely outside mainstream society. At the end of the
novel, with the assistance of some local Native Americans, she has
escaped the facility, made her way to the other end of the country,
and married another Native American. She is expecting a child, and
the reader is left at the end of the novel wondering what sort of child
it will be. It will be human, but will this new human force an expan-
sion of thought and emotion about what that means?

Like Gonzales and the editors of *The Great Ape Project*, Cary
Wolf has linked the problem of animal rights with the perennial
problem of human rights:

> because the discourse of speciesism... can be used to mark
> *any* social other, we need to understand that the ethical and
> philosophical urgency of confronting the institution of spe-
> ciesism and crafting a posthumanist theory of the subject *has
> nothing to do with whether you like animals*. We all, human and
> nonhuman animals alike, have a stake in the discourse...(7)

In Gonzales's novel, the powers arrayed against Lucy understand this point, at least. Jenny, Lucy's adoptive mother, realizes that
at a moment in history when even children are imprisoned at Guan-
tanamo and Abu Graib, the rights of a hybrid bonobo-human from
Congo must be vulnerable indeed.

Humans share almost 99 percent of our DNA with bonobos
and chimpanzees. We are as closely related to both species as they
are to each other, and we share important behaviors with both. Jared
Diamond, a contributor to *The Great Ape Project*, argues for revising
scientific nomenclature to reflect that similarity. Like Wolfe, the
whole volume by Singer and Cavalieri suggests that protecting the
great apes' basic rights is doubly obligatory, for it is a necessary step
in the process of freeing our own species, too, once and for all, from
domination and exploitation of the weak by the powerful.

And so we come back to Vercors. My title, "An Unnatural History," comes from an article by Susan McHugh, who suggests that a

"looming disciplinary crisis" is brought into focus by the new field of animal studies, a field that is textual and epistemological (488) rather than purely scientific. In the analysis of science historian Donna Haraway, taxonomies are intellectual technologies or tests for imposing convenient order and clarity; they do not necessarily reflect truth or even fact (253). All such tests, Vercors suggests—morphological, genetic, and reproductive—are inconclusive when applied to the human animal. So perhaps the best English title for *Les Animaux Denatures* is "you shall know them," a quotation from Jesus's parable of the tree and the fruit: it is action and behavior, he teaches, the existential rather than the essential, which, according to this parable *and* Vercors' novel, determine one's identity.

But humanity is also an exclusive club, as the genial old judge points out after Templemore's trial: human beings get to decide who is human. That being the case, Vercors seems to suggest, definitions should be inclusive rather than exclusive. All the tropis are human because *some* of them are. Lucy is human because her DNA includes some of Stone's genes as well as a bonobo's. And we humans are, in Jared Diamond's phrase, "the third chimpanzee," genetically and behaviorally varieties of the same thing, as perhaps a truly "natural" history would instruct us.

Works Cited

Cavalieri, Paola and Peter Singer. *The Great Ape Project: Equality beyond Humanity.* NY: St. Martin's Griffin, 1993.

Diamond, Jared. "The Third Chimpanzee" in *The Great Ape Project: Equality beyond Humanity.* 88-101.

Gonzales, Laurence. *Lucy: A Novel.* NY: Knopf, 2010.

Haraway, Donna. "Race: Universal Donors in a Vampire Culture. It's All in the Family: Biological Kinship Categories in the Twentieth-Century United States." *The Haraway Reader.* NY: Routledge, 2004. 251-93.

Hobsbawm, Eric. *The Age of Empire: 1875-1914.* NY: Vintage, 1989.

McHugh, Susan. "Literary Animal Agents," PMLA 124.2 (March 2009): 487-95.

Nussbaum, Martha. "The Moral Status of Animals." *Chronicle of Higher Education.* 3 Feb. 2006. B6-B8.

Vercors. *The Murder of the Missing Link.* Trans. Rita Barisse. NY: Pocket Books, 1955.

Wolfe, Cary. *Animal Rites: American Culture, the Discourse of Species, and Posthumanist Theory*. Chicago: University of Chicago Press, 2003.

IV: APPROACHES TO TEACHING LANGUAGE AND CULTURE

INSTRUCTIONAL UNITS INFORMED BY BACKWARD DESIGN

Eva-Maria Russo

In my position as a specialist in foreign language pedagogy, I often reflect on the most effective strategies to share with my graduate student colleagues, those which I would encourage graduate instructors to employ in their own classrooms to facilitate the most successful achievement of expected language learning outcomes. One great challenge to making such suggestions stems from what Kumaravadivelu labels as the present location of the field of language teaching in a "post-method condition" (qtd. in Larsen-Freeman and Freeman 164). Even the widespread popularity of the communicative language teaching approach does not equate to a single identifiable manifestation of effective instruction in the classroom. In addition to the multitude of available approaches, I keep in mind, and tend to agree with, the abundant evidence cited by Diane Larsen-Freeman and Daniel Freeman that demonstrates that "teachers' classroom practices are highly individual and durable" and that "attempts to impose a standard or uniform way of acting are likely to fail" (164). Teachers enter their classrooms with their own perceptions– whether consciously or unconsciously accumulated – as to how learning takes place, as well as their own personalities which determine in large part how they interact with their students. The importance of personality is not to be underestimated, as evidenced by such research as that performed by Monika Chavez in the Spring 1998 third- and fourth-semester German courses at University of Wisconsin-Madison. According to this research, characteristics such as "enthusiastic, interesting, fun, friendly, caring and helpful" were rated as more desirable in a teaching assistant than even knowledge of German or organizational skills (116). Of course variable personal time and energy commitment to instructional preparation also plays a role in an instructor's success in the classroom in guiding language acquisition, along with an instructor's employment of new and innovative strategies.

There are nonetheless some guidelines to which we may turn both in terms of the "what" and the "how" to teach – guidelines which, when considered in conjunction with one another, can assist instructors in composing logical syllabi with thematic units composed of scaffolded instruction as well as units that spiral. To start with a few useful definitions, by spiraling I refer to lessons that allow for an acquisition of new knowledge and skills based upon existing knowledge and experience, for learning from new sources and for the implementation of what has been learned. Spiraling hopefully occurs over the course of the semester but also over the course of successive levels, as a theme or language rule is revisited with ever-increasing complexity, facilitating the development of deeper comprehension. Scaffolded instruction, a teaching strategy grounded in Lev Vygotsky's sociocultural theory and his concept of the zone of proximal development,[1] structures individual instructional tasks in order to help students reach the next level of proficiency. It offers a motivational context at least to stimulate student interest and at best to convince students that the subject matter is pertinent for their own personal and professional development; it simplifies complex tasks by breaking them into more manageable steps which build upon previously-existing knowledge; it practices the thought process with students through "think aloud" talk and it provides language assistance to get students on the right track with their own production, etc. Finally the most convincing guidelines are to be located in backward design, the subject of my talk today and my most consistent suggestion within my own program.

I see Backward Design very clearly as a model for both curricular development and daily classroom practice that supplements the macro-guidelines provided by the ACTFL National Standards and Proficiency Guidelines as well as the Common European Framework of Reference and LinguaFolio. Since Backward Design is about first starting with your goals and working backward to content and strategies and the Standards and CEFR do set goals for language proficiency, these will serve as my starting point today. The ACTFL National Standards call upon instructors to familiarize students with more than just the functions of linguistic structures and vocabulary items; students are to connect the ability to communicate to a

---

[1] "For Vygotsky the ZPD embodies a concept of readiness to learn that emphasises [sic] upper levels of competence. These upper boundaries are not immutable, however, but constantly changing with the learner's increasing cultural competence. What a child can perform today with assistance she will be able to perform tomorrow independently, thus preparing her for entry into a new and more demanding collaboration" (Daniels 27).

knowledge und understanding of the new culture, to connections with other disciplines, and to a participation in multilingual communities at home and abroad in order to permit for comparisons of the native and target language and culture. Rather than referring to the four skills of listening, reading, writing and speaking as discrete entities within a cultural context, instructors are encouraged now to cycle students through the three modes of communication (interpretive, interpersonal and presentational) which simultaneously train multiple skills. On the website for the Center for Advanced Research on Language Acquisition (CARLA), instructors find a suggested example of one typical lesson which allows for the utilization of all three modes of communication – the creation of a "travel brochure or poster about a city or country where the target language is spoken" ("Assess 3 Modes"). Tasks are then described according to the cyclical "Performance Assessment Unit" defined in the ACTFL Integrated Performance Assessment but specific structuring of the tasks is only briefly outlined. Students start with the interpretive communication in this particular model as they "listen to or read an authentic text (e.g., newspaper article, radio broadcast, etc.) and answer information as well as interpretive questions to assess their comprehension of the material." They are introduced to some input about the subject matter so that subsequent production is not based on opinion alone and the teacher can already "provide students with feedback on their performance" at this point. Students then "[engage] in interpersonal oral communication about a particular topic which relates to the interpretive text;" one example might be a conversation about the city, perhaps what they would recommend visiting, when, why, and how. Finally "students engage in presentational communication by verbally sharing the research/ideas/opinions. Sample presentational formats [include] speeches, drama, skits, radio broadcasts, posters, brochures, essays, websites, etc." (Glisan et al. 18). Instructors might also note at this point that it would be quite simple to start with interpersonal as opposed to interpretive communication by means of an interview, during which students question one another about their pre-existing knowledge on the city or country.

If we keep in mind what instructors and/ or researchers are attempting to accomplish when seeking to fulfill the standards when all goals are considered to be equally important, while keeping a lesson manageable and engaging for students, ensuring that the students do the greatest amount of speaking, we see that this is certainly a demanding undertaking and it is not surprising that much criticism has been leveled both at instructional projects and textbooks for not getting it quite right. Consider the Web-based inquiry project conducted by Levi-Altstaedter and Jones, which tasked students with the design of just such a brochure, the creation of a concept map (a graphical tool for organizing and representing knowledge) and the composition of a reflective essay, all about an imaginary trip to Argentina (645). The description of the task was a familiar one, potentially meaningful in terms of the exposure to real rather than constructed content and in light of the authors' determination of the list of websites for student evaluation. The research study was nonetheless disparaged for promoting sites that presented trivializing facts on food, lodging, airlines, sports, etc -- all broadly "applicable to [...] all Latin American countries" (Wu 561). The criticism was therefore not so much directed toward the what – the employment of a project itself – but toward the realization of this project and, of course, its outcomes. Rather than acknowledging differences between the target culture and their own, student participants saw just similarities. What they learned was "multiculturalism – that is, a tolerance for different peoples and their cultures," a praiseworthy goal indeed, but not quite reaching that level of comprehension and production which we would like to achieve (Wu 562). Similar projects can be found in most textbooks out on the market today – projects which will expose students to some sort of authentic materials and demand their production of language, but projects which are nonetheless lacking – lacking in terms of the "high-quality," "critical," non-stereotyping knowledge about the target language and culture (Wu 561), and lacking in terms of the scaffolding steps that are incorporated to prepare the students to contribute progressively improved language, which sounds or reads less like a direct translation from the native language. While the ACTFL Proficiency Guidelines were created to help describe and assess what individuals can do with language "in terms of speaking, writing, listening, and reading in real-world situations in a spontaneous and non-rehearsed context" and have been revised for 2012 (and now define ability with reading and listening skills at 5 rather than 4 different levels of proficiency: Distinguished, Superior, Advanced, Intermediate, and Novice, with the major levels Advanced, Intermediate, and Novice still subdivided into High, Mid, and Low sublevels), we are reminded that they are "an instrument for the evaluation of functional language ability" ("ACTFL" 3). The purpose of the Guidelines is therewith clearly defined as a tool of assessment as opposed to a clarification of how students acquire the described levels or a recommendation of a particular pedagogical method, approach or educational curriculum to be employed. While ACTFL cautions that the standards "should not be used as a curriculum guide" nor should they dictate content (Mikulec and Chamness Miller 82), they can still help point instructors in the right direction regarding desired and achievable outcomes.

The major influence of the Common European Framework of Reference to the current point has similarly been found in the area of assessment (qtd. in Jones and Saville 53) and it too has faced its share of criticism on the basis of difficulty and a lack of preparation on the part of instructors attempting to use it, but its promise is also evident. Chapter 7 of the document actually promotes a defined instructional practice – specifically, task-based instruction – with tasks defined in the usual range from creative story writing to routine transactions at the bank or bakery, to presentations. In a manner reminiscent of Michael Long's needs analysis, the CEFR calls for "'real-life', 'target' or rehearsal tasks that are chosen on the basis of learners' needs outside the classroom, whether in the personal and public domains, or related to more specific occupational or educational needs" (Council of Europe 157). Certainly the same concerns arise with these guidelines as with Michael Long's recommendations. Do or can we always know what students' needs are before we design our syllabi? Many enter our classroom for the enjoyment of language learning (as evidenced by the results of the attitudinal survey that we administer at Washington University in St. Louis) rather than having a specific use for the language in mind. While chapter 7 of the CEFR does not lay out a sample lesson plan in keeping with the definitions of task-based instruction —in other words, a task which gives students partial ownership of the project; extends over several days, weeks or months; integrates skills; and develops students' understanding of a topic through the integration of language and content— the CEFR does address the subjects of time on task (163), considerations of text characteristics (165), the range of responses — from the non-verbal to spoken and written — that might be elicited (166), etc. More so than via the guidelines of this particular chapter, the employment of CEFR with its 34 descriptive scales for different communicative language activities (North 656) in the classroom is more readily realized by virtue of the European Language Portfolio or its American counterpart LinguaFolio (built on knowledge and insights gleaned from the European case studies and experiences with the

European Language Portfolio). A copy of the latter may be located on the website of the National Council of State Supervisors for Languages (NCSSFL). LinguaFolio is comprised of three parts: the Language Biography, which details a student's history and current encounters with language as well as their "learning habits and strategies"; the Language Passport, for which students describe and detail their own competence and proficiencies with the language, attained either formally or informally, by employing "can do" statements; and the Dossier of Evidence, in which students provide examples of their work, which they can trade in and out of their file. These documents then "serve as evidence of accomplishment of learning goals" (Moeller, Theiler and Wu 4-5). Looking at these individual sections, we already see the potential for agency on the part of the student; the student is called upon to reflect on a regular basis on progress made and to associate this with effort expended and results produced. The success of the employment of LinguaFolio has been documented at the secondary level, most recently in a longitudinal study conducted in Spanish courses in Nebraska, during which students' goal-setting processes and language proficiency performance were analyzed over 4 consecutive years. Recently I had the opportunity to speak to one of the authors of this study, who glowed in the successful conclusion of a five-year study, the resulting data of which revealed "a consistent increase in goal setting, action plan and reflection mean, [at least] from level 1 through level 3 of Spanish" (Moeller, Theiler and Wu 7). She eagerly laid out plans for the next research study: the determination of what teacher differences had to do with varied STAMP outcomes – that is that Standards Based Measurement of Proficiency, a foreign language test. The next step of the process thus lay, in her opinion, in the determination of those characteristics which made some instructors more successful than others.

In my 11 years of observational experience, the instructor, who is most successful in drawing students into a classroom lesson and in inspiring their time investment outside the classroom, is he or she with a desire and ability to truly engage students with a topic, to engage with the students themselves and with a meaningfully-constructed plan of action. One of the most effective curriculum designs has been shown to be the "backward design" model, as laid out by McTighe and Wiggins in their text *Understanding by Design*, revised in 2005. This type of curriculum design has been described as "backward," because instead of starting, as teachers traditionally would when planning a curriculum, with interesting activities and textbooks, in the backward design model the teacher starts with the end, the "desired results," and then derives the curriculum from the evidence of learning called for by the expectations and the "intellectual scaffolding" needed to equip students to produce and comprehend language. This means that we as instructors seek first to define with all transparency which essential understandings and proficiencies a student should achieve as a result of any plan (no matter the individual instructors' personalities) and regardless of any limitations that we face (Wiggins and McTighe 14-21).

It is important to note that the determination of acceptable evidence of comprehension and proficiency is not the equivalent of teaching toward a test; backward design does not have as its goal the mastery of discrete items or the coverage of certain grammatical points and vocabulary lists. We are moving away even from traditional content-focused design whereby the instructor would pick a topic, select a resource or resources which clearly exemplify this topic and then choose instructional methods based upon these resources, in the hopes of causing learning. Backward design is far more deliberate. By establishing what would be accepted as evidence that students have attained the desired understanding and proficiencies before proceeding to plan teaching and learning experiences, instructors are better able to remain focused on the desired results at all instructional levels, and to revise strategies as necessary over the course of the unit's implementation. For example, one topic addressed in our second-semester course is professions. It is a topic which can be found in many first-year textbooks and which can be considered relevant to and by students for whom the content is current as they apply for internship positions, etc. over the course of their academic career and some who even apply for a position in Germany, as one of my advisees just did. My goal is not just the introduction of job-related vocabulary, the reading of a German job ad or a cultural comparison of a German vs. an American resume. Rather my end-goal (a performance task) is student participation in a level-appropriate job interview. Keeping in mind the description of spoken production of the CEFR self-assessment grid for the A2-level, a basic job interview (as opposed to one for a specific position) will direct the students to learn and produce "a series of phrases and sentences to describe [... their] educational background, [their] present or most recent job" and to recycle descriptions of themselves as well as what they would like to achieve in a future position (Council of Europe 26). We seek to answer together the essential question of how students would market themselves in the native vs. the target culture. For the non-native speaker such as myself, who has never been interviewed for a job in Germany, it is possible nonetheless to inform oneself of the realities of the job interview by virtue of websites such as Staufenbiel.de, Focus.de with its list of "die fiesesten Fragen" and Bewerbung.de, which addresses acceptable questions since the passing of the *Allgemeine Gleichbehandlungsgesetz* in August of 2006.

Once desired results have been identified and acceptable evidence has been determined, then the instructor plans learning experiences and instruction. To achieve familiarity with the topic, "understandings" (Wiggins and McTighe 23) are scaffolded for the students over the course of somewhat more than three weeks. Students start by reviewing their course of studies and what led them to study their major or majors and minor at Washington University in St. Louis. They learn the names of various professions and what sort of work one completes or what qualities are most desirable in these professions. Student interest is "hooked" with the incorporation of authentic realia (resumes and job ads), their involvement in the discussion of the appropriateness of questions regarding religion, marital status and pregnancy, and by means of intermittent assessments. At regular intervals determined by the flow of the conversation, students are prompted to contribute suggestions as to how the new information would logically be included into a job interview. Informal checks/formative assessments are thus routinely integrated into the class, ranging from an image review of personal characteristics to a class favorite: the fast-paced mock-interview performed with a team of interviewers facing off against a team of interviewees. Such checks call upon students to check their own progress with both asking and answering questions on skills that they have, personal development toward which they strive, service that they can provide and job benefits that they seek to attain. At this point they can "rethink and revise" their understandings (Wiggins and McTighe 22).

Those who read Wiggins and McTighe's text should not get the impression that these design considerations are to be restricted to the lower-level classroom; the multifaceted view espoused by *Understanding by Design* of what comprises a mature understanding of a subject is of great assistance when determining that learning of content which is our goal in a higher-level course as well. A student with a true understanding can explain the topic under discussion by means of thorough, supported facts and data; can interpret and apply a topic (using it in diverse contexts); and can maintain perspective, empathize and have self-knowledge about the prejudices, projections and thought processes that both shape and impede their own understanding (Wiggins and McTighe 85-103). These same considerations accompany my treatment of one of the most challenging topics in the foreign language classroom: humor. In my fifth-semester course, I tackle the topic of humor in conjunction with the subject of *Karneval* in an effort to lay that essential question to rest: Is there any truth to the stereotype that Germans have little understanding (or a distorted understanding) of humorous situations? The performance task, which is students' end goal in this unit, is their production of a modified version of a *Büttenrede*, a carnival speech. Over the course of this unit, students are introduced to examples of that dialect that makes many carnival speeches inaccessible to a non-native audience, identifying how phonemes are modified in the dialect, enjoying the melodious sing-song of *Kölsch*; they watch sample excerpts from two *Karneval* speakers who employ somewhat more manageable language (Bernd Stelter and Marc Metzger) in order to identify the humorous techniques employed by a *Büttenredner* (exaggeration, anecdotes about local and international occurrences and personages, word play, etc.); they try their hand at joke writing (acknowledging the humor available in homonyms, recording everyday situations from their own lives as well as from headlines which can be twisted for the sake of humor, supplying set-ups for provided punchlines, and the like). While students write their own *Büttenrede* completely aware that they cannot master the style of the traditional carnival speech, there is value to this awareness of cultural difference and that the difference is not to be equated with some deficiency in the target culture.

In my pedagogy course this semester, I found myself recently confronted with the question of a graduate student who wondered why we discussed different theories and methods of foreign language instruction, if these were to be replaced after just a few years with a new approach that found favor with researchers and/or instructors. Hopefully what I have presented today is a talk that contributes to an understanding of how various scales and instructional design considerations actually can complement one another. Rather than discarding strategies as outdated or ineffective, instructors need to continue to increase their knowledge of strategies and reflect upon which should be incorporated in order that students gain the key knowledge and proficiencies that are the goals of each unit which comprises our curriculum.

Works Cited

"ACTFL Proficiency Guidelines 2012." American Council on the Teaching of Foreign Languages, 2 June 2012. <http://www.actfl.org/files/public/ACTFLProficiencyGuidelin es2012_FINAL.pdf>.

Center for Advanced Research on Language Acquisition. "Assess 3 Modes." *Modes of Communication*. N.p., n.d. 2 June 2012. <http://www.carla.umn.edu>.

Chavez, Monika. "Judgment Day: Students' Perspectives on End-of-Course Evaluations." *Die Unterrichtspraxis/Teaching German* 33.2 (2000): 113-124.

Council of Europe. "Common European Framework of Reference." Cambridge University Press, 2 June 2012. <http://www.coe.int/t/dg4/linguistic/Source/Framework_en. pdf>.

Daniels, Harry. "Vygotsky and Inclusion." *Psychology for Inclusive Education: New directions in theory and practice.* London: New York: Routledge, 2009. 24-37.

Glisan, Eileen, Bonnie Adair-Hauck, Keiko Koda, S. Paul Sandrock, and Elvira Swender. *ACTFL Integrated Performance Assessment.* New York: American Council on the Teaching of Foreign Languages, 2003.

Jones, Neil, and Nick Saville. "European Language Policy: Assessment, Learning, and the CEFR." *Annual Review of Applied Linguistics* 29 (2009): 51-63.

Larsen-Freeman, Diane, and Donald Freeman. "Language Moves: The Place of "Foreign Languages in Classroom Teaching and Learning." *Review of Research in Education* 32 (2008): 147-185.

Levi Altstaedter, Laura, and Brett Jones. "Motivating students' foreign language and culture acquisition through Web-based inquiry." *Foreign Language Annals* 42.4 (2009): 640-657.

Mikulec, Erin, and Paul Chamness Miller. "Using Project-Based Instruction to Meet Foreign Language Standards." *The Clearing House* 84.3 (2011): 81-86.

Moeller, Aleidine J., Janine M. Theiler, and Chaorong Wu. "Goal Setting and Student Achievement: A Longitudinal Study." *The Modern Language Journal* (2011): 1-17.

North, Brian. "The CEFR Illustrative Descriptor Scales." *The Modern Language Journal* 91.4 (2007): 656-659.

Wiggins, Grant, and Jay McTighe. *Understanding by Design.* 2nd ed. Alexandria, VA: Association for Supervision and Curriculum Development, 2005.

Wu, Ping. "The National Standards for Foreign Language Learning: Where's the Beef? A Response to 'Motivating Student's Foreign Language and Culture Acquisition through Web-Inquiry' by Levi Altstaedter & Jones." *Foreign Language Annals* 43.4 (2010): 559-562.

ACHIEVING THE LEAP REPORT'S ESSENTIAL LEARNING OUTCOMES THROUGH SERVICE-LEARNING IN FOREIGN LANGUAGE PEDAGOGY

Gabriel Ignacio Barreneche

The National Leadership Council for Liberal Education and America's Promise's (LEAP) 2007 report titled *College Learning for the New Global Century* states that one of the four Essential Learning Outcomes for college and university students is "Personal and Social Responsibility, including civic knowledge and engagement—local and global, intercultural knowledge and competence, ethical reasoning and action, and foundations and skills for lifelong learning (anchored through active involvement with diverse communities and real-world challenges)" (3). The LEAP report asks institutions of higher education to seek out teaching methodologies and curricula that can address these Essential Learning Outcomes and better prepare students to succeed in an increasingly interdependent and globalized world. Over the past decade, the use of academic service-learning and community-based learning has spread across campuses throughout the nation, with copious research in this field demonstrating the effectiveness of this approach to engaged learning. These high-impact practices have the capacity to assist college and university students in achieving the LEAP learning outcomes and better prepare them for success in the new millennium.[1]

Given the current climate in higher education and its increasing utilization of service-learning as a tool for student learning, foreign language programs face the challenge of contributing to their institution's achievement of the student learning outcomes proposed by the LEAP report. This paper will examine two examples where language students engaged in community service-learning projects enhanced their linguistic abilities and achieved some of these LEAP learning outcomes through teaching the target language and teaching in the target language. The first case study describes how advanced-level Spanish students at Rollins College have improved their speaking abilities through a partnership with Junior Achievement of Central

---

[1] For details on all of the high-impact practices in higher education, see Kuh (2008).

Florida (JA), teaching the JA curriculum to bilingual elementary school students in Spanish. The second case study illustrates how intermediate-level students of Spanish at Rollins enhanced their knowledge of the language by creating and teaching a beginner's Spanish conversation course for a group of senior citizens at the local public library. Using survey data and pre and post service assessments, we will see that community-engagement projects in language courses such as these can yield target language acquisition as well as achieve learning outcomes related to personal and social responsibility, as posited by the LEAP report.

Research in Service-Learning and Language

The National Service-Learning Clearinghouse defines service-learning as "… a teaching and learning strategy that integrates meaningful community service with instruction and reflection to enrich the learning experience, teach civic responsibility, and strengthen communities," a definition that highlights both the link between the academic course goals and the service activity as well as the civic learning component of this pedagogy.[2] Service-learning is employed in academic disciplines across campus, from the humanities to the natural sciences.[3] Growing research in the field of service-learning and community engagement has demonstrated both the benefits and limitations of applying this pedagogical approach to foreign language instruction.[4] Scholars and practitioners of service-learning pedagogy in language instruction have made connections between the national standard, the "5 Cs" of language learning (Lear & Abbott 2008),

---

[2] Given the narrow scope of this study, we will use the term "service-learning" rather than the broader term "community-based learning" (CBL), which refers to experiential academic activities rooted in the community that may not necessarily provide a service to the community partner.

[3] For a thorough discussion of best practices in service-learning and more extensive definitions, see Astin, Vogelgesang, Ikeda, and Yee (2000), Eyler and Giles (1999), Bringle and Hatcher (1995), Ash, Clayton, and Atkinson (2005) and Hatcher, Bringle, and Muthiah (2004), among others.

[4] Research in the field has appeared in leading academic journals such as *Foreign Language Annals*, *Hispania*, and the *Michigan Journal of Community Service Learning*, in addition to edited volumes on the subject published by Hellebrandt, Arries, and Varona (2004), and Wurr and Hellebrandt (2007). Furthermore, in 2013 *Hispania* will publish a special focus issue dedicated to the scholarship of community engagement.

measured the linguistic gains by language students in community-based learning courses (Pellettieri 2011), and studied the impact of service-learning on the motivation of language learners (Pak 2007) and their attitude towards the cultures of native Spanish speakers (Zapata 2011). Although advances have been made in the research in the field, opportunities for continued study and investigation still exist.

Rollins College – Junion Achievement Project

Since 2006, students in an advanced-level Spanish language course offered at Rollins College have partnered with non-profit community educators Junior Achievement of Central Florida. The course, titled Spanish for Advanced Communication (SPN 302), targets students mostly in their fifth semester of language study, and focuses on written and oral communication. With the goal of fine tuning students' writing and speaking abilities in the language, as well as broadening their vocabulary and polishing their pronunciation, the course requires students to interact and engage with native speakers of Spanish in the Orlando region through the partnership with Junior Achievement (JA).[5] Over the course of the semester, the Rollins students are responsible for preparing and teaching five lessons, in Spanish, from Junior Achievement's curriculum of basic economics, entrepreneurship, and community development for elementary-school students. Although JA provides all of the materials and lesson plans, Rollins students must translate these into Spanish and deliver the lessons to students in English as a Second Language programs around the city. In accordance with best practices in service-learning, the students are also required to write weekly reflection pieces and analysis of their service experience in Spanish.

Rollins College – Winter Park Library Project

In 2010 and 2011, students from Rollins College's first-year seminar program, the Rollins College Conference (RCC) put their Spanish skills to use for the benefit of their new community. These students, enrolled in Intermediate Spanish Conversation (SPN 210-S) sections

---

[5] See Barreneche (2011) for more details and analysis of the Rollins College-Junior Achievement partnership, as well as student reflections on the experience.

of the RCC program, partnered with the Winter Park Library and offered 10-week elementary Spanish conversation courses for members of the library's Lifelong Learning Institute, most of whom were senior citizens from the area. With guidance from their professors as well as from their upper-classmen Peer Mentors, these first-year students developed and implemented the weekly Spanish language course. The class included conversational topics such as greetings, vocabulary, formulating questions, talking about oneself and one's family, food and culture, among other topics. In the 2010 course, the number of community participants was small enough to allow for one-on-one and small group work to reinforce the topics presented in class. As with Spanish for Advanced Communication, the SPN 210-S course objectives included vocabulary development, as well as improving oral and written proficiency in the language. Similarly, students were required to produce written reflections on the experiences of teaching, curriculum development, and more broadly on the importance of giving of one's time and talents to the greater community, all in the target language.

Methodology

In order to measure both the linguistic gains as well as the achievement of LEAP learning outcomes, both the Junior Achievement and Winter Park Library projects employed survey data as well as assessment testing. As a way of evaluating progress in student language learning, all students of Spanish at Rollins College take the WebCAPE foreign language placement exam at the start and end of the semester. Because of this practice, the department can compare the linguistic gains of students in regular language courses with those who are participating in community-based learning projects such as JA and the Winter Park Library. Although it is useful for quickly identifying the language level of students across the Spanish program, the WebCAPE instrument has its limitations and is not a failsafe indicator of student language acquisition. First of all, it is a completely web-based multiple choice assessment that does not require students to write nor speak in the target language. Secondly, students are asked to take the assessment outside of class time, which implies a lack of uniform of test-taking conditions that may affect student scores. Finally, the variety of teaching styles among the faculty in the program could result in different scores between the control group sections of SPN 210-S, and the first-year seminar with the service-learning component.[6]

Progress towards achieving the LEAP learning outcomes from these two service-learning projects was also documented. Rollins' Office of Community Engagement conducted in-class surveys of all students involved in both the JA and Winter Park Library projects. These surveys queried the students' previous levels of involvement in community engagement activities, their perspectives on the importance of participating in the local community, their thoughts on linking academic major programs and work in the community, as well as specific questions targeting their own assessment of their achievement of the LEAP outcomes related to civic knowledge and engagement, personal and social responsibility, and knowledge of human cultures. Because they did not have a community-engagement component to the course, these surveys were not conducted in other sections of SPN 210-S, and there were no other sections of SPN 302 offered in the years during this study. As such, there were no control groups to which one could compare the LEAP learning outcomes of students not participating in a service-learning project. It is important to note that the designers of these projects do not expect students to instantly transform from novices in community engagement to community activists. These courses are intended to serve as a component of a continuum of learning and student engagement that should take place over the academic careers of the students and through several academic activities and co-curricular experiences.

Outcomes

I. WebCAPE

As discussed earlier, the results from the student WebCAPE assessments for the JA project could not be used in a comparative study due to the lack of a control group for the SPN 302 course. As such, the WebCAPE results could not establish if students acquired more language skills directly as a result of the JA project. This is an area that warrants further study and could advance the case for increased integration of service-learning projects as part of the curricula of foreign language programs at the university level.

---

[6] It is important to note that the first-year seminars and all other sections of SPN 210-S shared the same curriculum and textbooks.

Because there were several sections of Intermediate Spanish Conversation (SPN 210-S) taught concurrently with the service-learning section (first-year seminar), we were able to compare WebCAPE results between sections. Additionally, in fall of 2010, the author of this study personally taught the service-learning section in addition to one regular section of SPN 210-S. All students of SPN 210-S and their service-learning section counterparts took the WebCAPE exam twice during the semester, once at the start, and again before final exams. Whereas the service-learning section noted an overall gain of 63.7, the same section of the same course taught by the same instructor recorded a gain of only 32.75 points. The difference between the service-learning section (11 students) when compared to all of the regular sections of 210-S (54 students) was similar. All regular sections of 210-S recorded a gain of 36.4 points. In 2011, the service-learning section of the course (11 students) scored an overall gain of 180.9 points, in comparison to all other sections of 210-S (48 students), with a gain of only 16.7 points.

Course	Average Gain WebCAPE
Fall 2010: service-learning section of SPN 210-S taught by author (11 students)	63.7
Fall 2010: regular section of SPN 210-S taught by author (13 students)	32.75
Fall 2010: all regular sections of SPN 210-S (54 students)	36.4
Fall 2011: service-learning section, SPN 210-S (11 students)	180.9
Fall 2011: all regular sections of SPN 210-S (48 students)	16.7

The data presented would convincingly suggest that the service-learning component of the course contributed to increasing the students' linguistic competency. However, as discussed earlier, the WebCAPE instrument is overly simple in its multiple choice format and fails to assess other areas of language competency, namely writing, listening comprehension, and oral language production. Secondly, the varied testing conditions and the students' previous knowledge of Spanish are not taken into consideration when the data sets are compared. Finally, with only a small number of students in the service-learning project sections, it would be difficult to conclude that service-learning is the "silver bullet" for improving student language capabilities.

II. Survey Data

During the 2010-2011 academic year, Rollins College's Office of Community Engagement conducted surveys of the SPN 302 course as well as the service-learning section of SPN 210-S to assess these courses' service projects and measure if student attitudes and perspectives shifted as a result of their work in the community. The anonymous respondents noted their level of agreement or disagreement with a total of 33 statements. Below are the responses to three measures of student attitudes towards service and community engagement.

"The community participation aspect of this course helped me to see how the subject matter I learned can be used in everyday life."	
SPN 302	88% agree or strongly agree
SPN 210-S	66% agree or strongly agree

"This work has helped me to acknowledge my Personal and Social Responsibility, including: Civic knowledge and engagement–local and global intercultural knowledge and competence, ethical reasoning and action, foundations and skills for lifelong learning."	
SPN 302	100% indicated "YES"
SPN 210-S	92% indicated "YES"

"Contributing to a larger community: This opportunity allowed me to acknowledge and act on my responsibility to the educational community, as well as my responsibility to the wider society, locally, nationally, and globally."	
SPN 302	88% agree or strongly agree
SPN 210-S	100% agree or strongly agree

The responses to these three statements in the survey indicate that, although not every student saw a clear connection between the course material and the service-learning project, an overwhelming majority believed that the activities enhanced their understanding of the importance of contributing to the larger community and indicated an increased awareness of personal and social responsibility. As mentioned earlier, LEAP learning outcomes are not to be achieved solely through one academic service-learning experience. Nonetheless, it is clear that a foreign language course with well-designed and integrated service-learning activities can function as one of several steps students take in achieving the goals articulated by the LEAP report.

III. Student Reflections

In addition to WebCAPE data and the survey conducted by the Office of Community Engagement, written student reflections also provide a valuable source of information regarding student learning outcomes. Student reflections from the Winter Park Library project indicated that, as a result of the experience teaching language, they improved their pronunciation, had a better understanding of some grammatical structures, and the project refreshed their memory of language basics that they had forgotten over the years. Furthermore, participating in this project increased their motivation to be a part of future community engagement initiatives on campus. In their reflective pieces, participants in the JA project also noted increased confidence in speaking in public in Spanish, a broader vocabulary base, improved comprehension of native speakers of Spanish, in addition to more motivation to continue language study because of the experience of using the language in a meaningful context with real interlocutors. Similarly, these students indicated an interest in participating future community engagement projects.[7]

Conclusions

As evidenced by the two service-learning projects described in this study, foreign language programs can use service-learning pedagogy and effective partnerships with local community agencies to help students achieve the learning outcomes that will prepare them for the challenges of a global society while increasing their linguistic competency. Furthermore, foreign language programs can be active participants in the service-learning movements on their campuses and demonstrate their importance in driving the institution's educational and social missions. On the one hand, the JA project model requires that students have access to a large population of native speakers of the target language, and as such it may not function well for many foreign language programs. On the other hand, the model presented by the Winter Park Library project can be duplicated by most any language program, provided there is an interest in the local community for learning that particular language. Furthermore, with an increasing elder population in our nation and research that illustrates that language learning and bilingualism can delay the effects of Alzheimer's disease and offset dementia (Bailystock 2011), non-profit organizations such as the Winter Park Library's Lifelong Learning Institute seek out opportunities for foreign language instruction, and students of any language can put their knowledge into practice while serving their communities. Although many variables and intangibles

---

[7] For excerpts from the JA student reflections, see Barreneche (2011).

exist in student learning of language, it is evident that by using the target language in rich and meaningful contexts, such as in the local community, students can gain linguistic skills as well as enhance their understanding of Personal and Social Responsibility as the AAC&U suggests. With creative course planning and effective community partnerships, language programs have the capacity to engage in high-impact practices that lead to student success in "College Learning for the New Global Century."

Works Cited

Ash, Sarah L., Clayton, Patti H., and Atkinson, Maxine P. "Integrating Reflection and Assessment to Capture and Improve Student Learning." *Michigan Journal of Community Service Learning* 11.2 (2005): 49–60.

Astin, Alexander W., Lori J. Vogelgesang, Elaine K. Ikeda, and Jennifer A. Yee. *How Service Learning Affects Students.* Los Angeles: U of California, Higher Education Research Institute, 2000.

Barreneche, Gabriel Ignacio. "Language Learners as Teachers: Integrating Service-learning and the Advanced Language Course." *Hispania* 94.1 (2011): 103-20.

Bialystok, Ellen. "Reshaping the Mind: The Benefits of Bilingualism." *Canadian Journal of Experimental Psychology* 65. 4 (2011): 229-35. 5 June 2012.

Bringle, Robert G. and Julie A. Hatcher. "A Service-Learning Curriculum for Faculty." *Michigan Journal of Community Service Learning* 2.1(1995): 112–22.

College Learning for the New Global Century. National Leadership Council for Liberal Education and America's Promise. Washington, DC: Association of American Colleges and Universities, 2007.

Eyler, Janet, and Dwight E. Giles, Jr. *Where's the Learning in Service-Learning?* San Francisco: Jossey-Bass, 1999.

Hatcher, Julie A., Robert G. Bringle, and Richard Muthiah. "Designing Effective Reflection: What Matters to Service-Learning?" *Michigan Journal of Community Service Learning* 11.1 (2004): 38–46.

Hellebrandt, Josef, Jonathan Arries, and Lucía T. Varona, eds. *Juntos: Community Partnerships in Spanish and Portuguese.* Boston: Thomson/Heinle, 2004.

Kuh, George D. *High-Impact Educational Practices: What They Are, Who Has Access to Them, and Why They Matter.* Washington, DC: Association of American Colleges and Universities, 2008.

Lear, Darcy W., and Annie R. Abbott. "Foreign Language Professional Standards and CSL: Achieving the 5 C's." *Michigan Journal of Community Service Learning* 14.2 (2008): 76–86.

Pak, Chin-Soo. "The Service-Learning Classroom and Motivational Strategies for Learning Spanish: Discoveries From Two Interdisciplinary Community-Centered Seminars." *Learning the Language of Global Citizenship: Service-Learning in Applied Linguistics.* Ed. Adrian J. Wurr and Josef Hellebrandt. Bolton, MA: Anker, 2007. 32–57.

Pellettieri, Jill. "Measuring Language-related Outcomes of Community-based Learning in Intermediate Spanish Courses." *Hispania* 94.2 (2011): 285–302.

"What Is Service-Learning?" National Service-Learning Clearinghouse. 6 June 2012.

Wurr, Adrian J., and Josef Hellebrandt, eds. *Learning the Language of Global Citizenship: Service-Learning in Applied Linguistics.* Bolton, Massachusetts: Anker, 2007.

Zapata, Gabriela. "The Effects of Community Service Learning Projects on L2 Learners' Cultural Understanding." *Hispania* 94.1 (2011): 86-102.

FROM ANALYTICAL TO ANALOGOUS THINKING: THE RELEVANCE OF TRANSNATIONAL APPROACHES

Heike Scharm

The optimism and fervor motivating present intellectual discourse regarding globalization and the celebration of multiculturalism stand in stark contrast with the political, academic, and social reality which continues to shape the first decades of the 21st century. Angela Merkel's, Nicolas Sarkozy's, and David Cameron's public announcements on the failure of Europe's "multikulti" [multicultural] society evoke Zygmunt Bauman's skepticism towards the possibility of a global community, which he bases on the inherent logistics of globalization itself. While the particularities of this common thread or "diagnosis" of our global era is nothing new in and of itself, it appears even more surprising that there still exists a blatant discrepancy between these present day realities, and the curriculum and teaching methodologies implemented in most U.S. Universities, especially in the humanities.

In light of this discrepancy, I would like to make a case for transnational and interdisciplinary approaches in the classroom. Much more than an academic fad, I see the fostering of analogous thinking and comparatist attitudes as a way to better prepare our students for the new challenges they will be facing in their lifetime, and to foster in them a mentality of global community builders. I will argue that by directing our students from the traditional, predominantly analytical and "insular" way of thinking towards analogous thought processes, we encourage them to question the conventional meaning of essence (and thus also of "cultural identities") as something immutable and *a priori* in a way that brings them closer to the postnational realities of the 21st century. While I do not pretend to offer a utopian solution to resolve the many conflicts globalization has caused or further complicated, I do consider a change in teaching approaches a first and necessary step towards the right direction. By adjusting not just the content of our curriculum but also the way we teach it, the classroom can become an invaluable contribution to the fostering of a dearly needed *trans*-national consciousness, in order to instill in our students a greater understanding and respect for otherness and to help them to recognize otherness as an inherent part of their own changing cultural identities.

From Aristotle to postmodernism, analytical thought has been the pillar of Western thinking. In Aristotle, analytical thought (from *ana* + *lyein*) is defined as a 'taking apart' or 'splitting up,' and as such has provided the foundation of the platonic method of *Diaeresis*. Analysis, in biology, refers to the dissection of organic tissue. A chirurgic process, it pretends to "de-construct" a whole —to literally disassemble it— in order to lay bare its composition and structure. In order to do so, analysis proceeds from the outside towards the inside, where one supposes to find the presence of an immutable essence (the "heart", the "root", the "bottom" of things). This essence is understood as the carrier of meaning and identity, its transcendental soul, if you will.

Notwithstanding the revolutionary impact of postmodern thought, Derridian deconstruction is still based predominantly on traditional analytical thought. A postmodern thinker continues to understand a subject as the total of its constituent parts and presupposes some kind of meaning at its center. Deconstruction peels away layer upon layer in the quest for the Holy Grail of rational thought: the essence of things. The fact that postmodernism demoted essence to an ever-evasive holder of meaning does not change nor even question the traditional structure of analytical thought. Although the postmodern thinker rejects the notion of absolute truths and argues, quite successfully, that ultimately meaning evades us, his way of reasoning still looks for answers within, still proceeds from the outside towards the inside and concerns itself primarily with the particular, such as the question of origins, the quest for roots, the vindication of the subaltern, the rehabilitation of a region, the identity of a nation, etc.. However, and despite its undeniable necessity and usefulness during the second part of the past century, postmodern thought processes have trained us (as we have trained our students) to overappreciate the value of essence, attainable or not, as the absolute carrier of meaning, as that which holds at its center the definition of its being, and as such its function, its absolute identity, in short, the designation of its *nature*.

Analogous or comparative approaches engage in a different kind of thought process. Analogy (from *analogia*, "proportion" or "relation") is a type of reasoning based on the correspondence between things of different origins. Analogous processes infer meaning from one particular subject to another by means of associations, comparisons, similarities in functions, and resemblances. Therefore, analogy relies on creativity, on perception, on emotive responses, and, most importantly, on acts of communication. While analysis proceeds from the outside to the inside (the disassembly of internal structures) and occupies itself with the particular (the self), analogy proceeds from the inside towards the outside (by means of associations) and is concerned with the universal (the self and/with the other).

The reason for this reversed direction and the preference for the universal over the particular is found in the way analogue thinking defines essence as a holder of meaning: while an analyst may engage in a process of dissection until he or she gets to a presupposed "root" (the meaning) of a thing or issue, an analogue thinker looks for meaning in the way the subject relates to the world around it. This could be done by means of comparison, or as practiced in the use of metaphors, parables, poetic discourse, etc. Rather than an immutable inner core, *essence* is now understood as a dynamic and ongoing process, which is "centered" within the points of connection between things, and hence becomes entirely dependent upon their correspondences, their exchanges with —and itineraries across— the outside world.

Analogous thought processes are, of course, not an invention of modern times —all to the contrary. Analogy was the tool of preference for pre-Socratic thinkers and continues to be widespread within Eastern thought, while analytical thinking has dominated rational Western thought and, as a consequence, shaped the characteristics of our modern world. Since the 19th Century, writers and philosophers have referred to the pathology of Western modernity, especially the crisis of meaning and the creation of the "lonely mass man". Indeed, one could argue that these two characteristics are intrinsically related, and as such, are especially poignant and fitting to describe our global society today.

Over the course of his long career, Octavio Paz defines modern man as disconnected from his world and the other. As he writes in his *Poetics of Convergence*, "before, man spoke with his universe; or he believed he did so [...]. In the 20th century, the mythical interlocutor and his voices have evaporated. Man has found himself alone in the immense city, and his loneliness is the loneliness of millions like him"

(508).[1] Likewise, Zygmunt Bauman speaks of the "disjunction" between man and his world. A sign of modern times, according to Bauman, man found himself "being neither inside nor outside [of his world], neither included nor excluded" (77). More than a century before the Mexican poet and the Polish sociologist, Nietzsche called attention to the same disconnect between modern man's interiority and exteriority. Interestingly enough, in his essay on the "Use and Abuse of History," Nietzsche draws a connection between modern man's "disjunction" and the way students are being taught to think and acquire knowledge. While the philosopher does not delve directly into a critical comparison between analytical versus analogous thought processes, he does so indirectly yet clearly, by first praising the thought process of the pre-Socratics ("Ancient People") while denouncing those practiced by modern Western society. Modern man, as Nietzsche writes,

> carries around an enormous amount of indigestible rocks of knowledge, which on occasion, make a considerable rumbling noise in his belly [...]. This rumbling reveals the true characteristic of modern man: the strange antithesis between an interior, which is lacking a correspondence to an exterior, and an exterior without correspondence to an interior, an antithesis not known by the ancient people [...]. [This type of knowledge] no longer possesses a transforming force pushing from the inside towards the outer world, but rather it stays hidden within a certain chaotic inner consciousness [...](132).[2]

---

[1] *Ruptura y convergencia*: "Antes, el hombre hablaba con el universo; o creía que hablaba: si no era su interlocutor era su espejo. En el siglo XX el interlocutor mítico y sus voces misteriosas se evaporan. El hombre se ha quedado solo en la ciudad inmensa y su soledad es la de millones como él." All translations are mine. Translated quotes are included as footnotes in their original language.

[2] Nietzsche's original quote, in its entirety, reads as follows: "Der moderne Mensch schleppt zuletzt eine ungeheure Menge von unverdaulichen Wissenssteinen mit sich herum, die dann bei Gelegenheit auch ordentlich im Leibe rumpeln, wie es im Märchen heißt. Durch dieses Rumpeln verrät sich die eigenste Eigenschaft dieses modernen Menschen: der merkwürdige Gegensatz eines Inneren, dem kein Äußeres, eines Äußeren, dem kein Inneres entspricht, ein Gegensatz, den die alten Völker nicht kennen. Das Wissen, das im Übermaße ohne Hunger, ja wider das Bedürfnis

This critical view on Western education and its consequences strongly resonates within the present state of higher education, and, ironically, especially within the humanities, where we tend to teach and analyze thought "inwardly", in a way that resembles the feeding of indigestible rocks, without applying the potentially transforming powers of analogous thought. Nietzsche warns that acquiring knowledge this way turns modern man into a savage savant. Nietzsche thus calls the product of Western education a walking encyclopedia, or a "Manual for an Inward Education for Outward Barbarians" ["Handbuch innerlicher Bildung für äußerliche Barbaren"] (133). Unidirectional, inward knowledge reinforces "this opposition between the inner and outer [which] makes the outer even more barbaric". The reason for this, as he explains, lies within the Western modern tradition of focusing on inward, isolating, thought processes, which look towards the center as the carrier of meaning. With prophetic clarity, Nietzsche considered this "inward" education detrimental to the intellectual and ethical formation of the individual, as well as to the shaping of a nation as a whole, because, as he argues, "when a people grows only from within and according to its own rudimentary needs", a nation will ultimately become barbaric (133)[3]. Isolated, "inward" knowledge does not teach to look beyond oneself, lacks the transforming powers pushing outward, and does not foster meaningful relations with the outside world.

While I do not wish to insinuate that our higher education models lead to the barbarization of our students or nation, Nietzsche does make a valid point that merits consideration, especially when applied to our present day global complexities. When Octavio Paz offered his pessimistic diagnosis of the pathologies of our modernity, he established a similar cause-and-effect between traditional thought processes directed inward, and modern man's disconnect with the

---

aufgenommen wird, wirkt jetzt nicht mehr als umgestaltendes, nach außen treibendes Motiv und bleibt in einer gewissen chaotischen Innenwelt verborgen, die jener moderne Mensch mit seltsamen Stolze als die ihm eigentümliche 'Innerlichkeit' bezeichnet" (132).
[3] " [...] und so ist die ganze moderne Bildung wesentlich innerlich: auswendig hat der Buchbinder so etwas daraufgedruckt wie 'Handbuch innerlicher Bildung für äußerliche Barbaren'. Ja dieser Gegensatz von innen und außen macht das Äußerliche noch barbarischer als es sein müßte, wenn ein rohes Volk nur aus sich heraus nach seinen derben Bedürfnissen wüchse".

outside world. He especially denounces the sacred value attached to Western individuality and to the pursuit of the self, which neglects the importance of the other in the shaping of one's own identity or self-fulfillment. Considering today's global mobility, the fact that an important part of our own students come from mixed heritages, and that many of them will come into contact with (and will be shaped by) other cultures, this idea of an "eigentümliche Innerlichkeit", or "unique interiority", as Nietzsche calls it, has lost its sense. As Paz explains, "wanting to be yourself means to condemn yourself to self-mutilation", since, as in analogous thinking, meaning can only be found with "the other" (259). This is a relevant observation, because for Paz, as for Nietzsche, there exists a strong connection between the way modern man thinks and learns, and the way he understands others and himself. Nietzsche sees this "inward" understanding as a path to a people's self-destruction, while Paz equates it to self-mutilation and in part responsible for the botched project of modernity, or, what Bauman calls our failed global community.

Interdisciplinary and transnational approaches function on the basis of analogous thinking. They offer a method of thought, which shifts the focus from interiority and uniqueness towards exteriority and correspondence, and replaces essence as an insular concept with the encounter and exchange with otherness. As a result, these approaches promote a different understanding of the self and the other, of their function and mutual dependency. Rewiring the brain could then lead first to the acceptance of the "ineradicable plurality of the world" (Bauman 98) —let's remember that analogies only function between two intrinsically *different* subjects. Second, as Bauman would like, it could then lead to tolerance, and finally, to solidarity (257). Thought processes based on analogies prepare this path, as they engage the quest for meaning not *within* the self, but *with* the "other", through exchange and collaboration, but only after recognizing and respecting its "otherness". Likewise, for Paz, analogy is a form of mediation. This kind of mediation "does not imply unity of the world [...] but rather its division" (397). An analogy as mediation (something is *as*, and not *is*) is only possible between two separate entities, or else it would eradicate differences and lead us back to the dangerous path of false universalisms or relativism, or, even worse, towards forced cultural assimilation (Merkels' idea of "multikulti").

Analogy is especially useful in the humanities and social sciences —disciplines whose goal consists of fostering a better understanding of human nature and cultures. In an essay defined as his "stab at intellectual bridge-building", Willis proposes to return to an understanding of higher education as an *initiation to life*. For this to be possible, Willis deems it necessary to start "from the perception that all our reasoning [...] are dialogues rather than isolated reasoning subjects" (60). As do transnational readings and interdisciplinary approaches, analogous thinking relies predominantly on dialogue. Applied to a wide range of subject matters, analogous thinking prepares our students to build "intellectual" and also transnational bridges, and therefore offers a fitting initiation to a life progressively more complex and multicultural. Teaching methods based on analogous thought aim to re-establish the communication between interiority (self, culture, nation) and exteriority (otherness perceived as relatable). The focus is to create points of contacts and correspondences and search for meaning within them. The search for rooted identity is therefore replaced with the search for analogies, while essence (the *nature* of things) only gains meaning as a dynamic process of change and exchange. The ultimate objective is to generate the capability to transgress the limits imposed by traditional curricula (one time-period, one field, one culture, one history, one language, one literary or artistic movement, etc.), in order to construct a base of knowledge and an understanding of the world that pushes outward, and thus, as Donskis states, furthers their capacity to "embrace other identities and forms of humanity" (166). If we can achieve this, higher education stands a chance to become an "initiation to life", and regains its transforming power. By relying on closed theory-to-practice-models, rather than open systems of thought, our education systems may be producing experts in their respective fields ("walking encyclopedia"), but we are far from fostering a mentality of global community builders.

Present day contexts and exigencies require different tools than those provided by modernism or even postmodernism. Our students are faced with challenges that require a change in mentality and thought processes. The urgency of approaches that foster bridge-building has intensified across various spheres of the artistic and intellectual community, and especially in higher education. Analogous thought processes meet this need for openness, for negotiation, for recognizing the world as a connective tissue with a common destination. By returning to a view of the universe as a model of interconnectivity and an understanding of human existence as Dasein, as defined by Heidegger as being-open-to-the-world, we could value interdisciplinary and transnational approaches in the classroom as a catalyst for global community building. While I do not suggest that analogies alone can change the world or human nature, teaching our students a different way of thinking could be a first step in regaining the transforming power of knowledge, in the Nietzschean sense, as a force pushing outward, in hopes to better prepare next generations to meet the challenges of a global society, and to inspire in them a stronger sense of solidarity for – and a sense of self *with* –the other.

Works Cited

Bauman Zygmunt. *Liquid Times. Living in an Age of Uncertainty.* Cambridge UK: Polity Press, 2010.

Donskis, Leonidas. *Troubled Identity and the Modern World.* New York: Palgrave MacMillan, 2009.

Nietzsche, Friedrich. *Werke in zwei Bänden.* Vol I. München: Carl Hanser Verlag, 1967.

Paz, Octavio. *Obras completas.* Vol. 1. Mexico: Círculo de lectores, 1997.

Willis, John. "The Post-Postmodern University". *Change* (March-April 1995): 59-62.

CPSIA information can be obtained
at www.ICGtesting.com
Printed in the USA
BVHW072217080121
597313BV00009B/126